Evan. J.

ECCENTRIC
The Life of Dr. William Price

by
DEAN POWELL

First Published 2005

ISBN 0-9550854-0-3

Published by
DEAN POWELL
4 The Mews, Church Street, Llantrisant
South Wales CF72 8SP

Copyright © 2005 by Dean Powell

All rights reserved.
No part of this work may be
reproduced, or stored in a retrieval system
or transmitted in any form or by any means,
electronic, mechanical, photocopying,
recording or otherwise,
without clearance from the publisher.

Dean Powell has asserted his moral right
under the Copyright, Design and Patents Act 1988
to be identified as author of this work.

DESIGNED & PRODUCED BY
GLENSIDE PRINTING
WATTSTOWN, PORTH, RHONDDA

Dedication

This book is dedicated with the utmost gratitude to three doctors whose lives were inextricably linked by their studies and years of service at The London Hospital, Whitechapel, and the profound effect they had on the life of the author, who underwent treatment there.

To Dr Michael Jones, for being the guiding light in leading the author's first, difficult steps. To Mr Brian Roper, a surgeon, friend and saviour, whose dedication and genius can never be truly repaid for guiding the author to a full and accomplished life. Finally, to old Dr Price himself, for inspiring the author as a child while growing up in the shadow of East Caerlan.

Contents

Foreword	1
The Boy	6
The Student	13
The Surgeon	27
The Chartist	43
The Archdruid	51
The Litigant	62
The Welshman	69
The Heretic	81
The Eccentric	96
The Passing	103
The Legacy	122

Foreword

CHARTIST, surgeon, heretic, Archdruid and pioneer in the legalisation of cremation in the British Isles, Dr William Price was undoubtedly one of the most flamboyant, romantic and eccentric characters in Welsh history, as bright and colourful as his burning funeral pyre which shone across a dark, Victorian age. Whether regarded as a figure born ahead of his time, or simply a certified madman prone to severe bouts of bizarre behaviour, there is no doubt that more than a century after his death he is still viewed with fascination for the beliefs which saw him both admired and persecuted throughout his 93 years.

He was a famed healer, Falstaffian rebel, crusader of reform, exiled political activist and a sparkling, dynamic, eloquent man who blazed progress and controversy by outraging a conventional society. Price, the complex individual, lived in a nonconformist, deacon-dominated Wales and succeeded in infuriating an entire population. Yet, his incredible legacy cannot be underestimated. The passing of the Cremation Act in 1902 had a profound effect on the entire country, but there was much more to Dr William Price than his radical attitudes to cremation. His entire life was filled with the most unimaginable events, usually outshone by the cremation of his infant child. Were those actions due to an honest distaste for human burial under hygienic grounds, or were his beliefs far deeper rooted in Druidic rituals of which he claimed to be the master scholar?

Whatever the reason, he still deserves record as the man whose deeds on a hilltop above the ancient town of Llantrisant caused a revolutionary result in a new method of disposal of the dead. His burning of the body of his son with full pagan rites, carried out like some intruder from Dante's Inferno, saw him stalk around the leaping flames, clothed in long Druidic robes, his tumbled white hair streaming in the wind, reciting incantations in Welsh over a burning casket. At the time, few would have realised the tremendous impact he would have on modern-day society. The criminal trial that followed aroused interest not only in Britain, but throughout the world.

Dr William Price's Cremation at East Caerlan in 1893.

As the most notable individual in 19th century Wales, Dr Price was far from the epitome of the Victorian gentleman, defying in the most exhibitory fashion the conventions and beliefs of his time including law, religion, morality and even his own medical profession. In his youth he practised nudism, roaming stark naked across the clouded mountains close to his home, attempting to bring back some form of a new Druidic society lost with the advent of Christianity in Britain.

Poverty-stricken in his youth, he hailed from a particularly troubled family, with an insane priest for a father and an illiterate maid for a mother. Remarkably, Price himself grew up to be a rather brilliant scholar, becoming a surgeon by the age of just 21. Sadly, few can dismiss claims that insanity prevailed, particularly during his latter years when, although many of his public speeches and writings were often lucid, they were equally as prone to totally preposterous statements. Coupled with his close friendships with gentlemen of equally outlandish ideologies, there is little doubt why Price was observed with as much fear as respect.

It must be remembered that Price was certainly not alone in his beliefs. His life, which spanned almost the entire century, came at a time when Wales was under serious threat of total obscurity from the might of the British Empire. It was a time when individuals fought for their national identity and culture. A time of forgery to recreate Welsh history, the growth of a Druidic ideology and an era of massive political activism.

After naming himself the Archdruid of Wales, this dignified adult claimed his first son would be the next Druidic ruler of the earth. It was a prophecy he claimed to have seen in the hieroglyphics of an ancient Greek stone in the Louvre while on exile in France. He believed that in becoming the first person in 2,000 years to interpret them, he had foreseen the future of the rise of the Druid people. In naming himself the Son of the Primitive Bard, a high order of Druid, Price adopted this new philosophy as his own, publishing those ideals in the most incomprehensible form of Welsh.

With eyes filled with fiery activity, he was a man bold enough to challenge existing beliefs and to defy conventions. He questioned the justice of the social system, poured scorn on orthodox religion, despised the law and its administrators, and decried the morality of a puritanical society. Courting controversy was as natural as the air he breathed and he displayed behaviour which shocked. A firm believer in vegetarianism, with a flair of compassion and vision, his renown as a healer was widespread, though it is doubtful his methods would meet with the approval of today's physicians. His great talent as a surgeon earned him extra fame, but he vehemently attacked the medical practices of Victoria's reign. His impressive generosity and his willingness to place his professional services gratuitously at the disposal of the poor, endeared him to the many who benefited from his skill. Price's medical reputation survives untarnished. Blunt and forthright to patients who would consult him when other more orthodox methods had failed, he fully supported alternative medicines, healthy living and fresh air, and refused to treat smokers.

He made one of the first attempts at creating an embryonic national health service, believing patients should pay him when they were well and he would treat them for free if they became ill. He performed a bone-graft operation on an injured worker and delivered the heir to an ironmaster's fortune by Caesarean section on a kitchen table. Fearless in support of the Welsh language and its culture, Dr Price also masterminded a major project to house a museum to Druidism and culture a century before today's Welsh Folk Museum attracts visitors by their thousands, a scheme which even saw the support of leading landowners of the day. Advocating free love, he was personally successful in this philosophy, having fathered illegitimate children throughout the district and standing on the Rocking Stone, or Y Maen Chwyf, in Pontypridd he would chant pagan addresses to the moon, much to the amusement of local non-believers. Dr Price was a leader in the failed Chartist rising of 1839, and, dressed as a woman, was forced to flee to France. Years later, when declared bankrupt following his building of two irregular-shaped houses in Pontypridd, he escaped the besieging police again, this time in a wooden chest which was carted out of the house and allowed him safe passage to Paris, where he remained in exile for years.

Evidently during his long lifetime Dr. Price was no stranger to the courts, both as a defendant and petitioner. He was charged with the manslaughter of a patient and had his father's body exhumed to prove mental illness, infuriating an entire community in doing so. Possessing an extensive knowledge of the law, and draped in a shawl of royal tartan, he would conduct his own defence brilliantly, lacing his speeches with a kind of mystic poetry. He satirically brought along to court as his learned counsel his infant daughter, whom he rather incredulously named Hiarlles Morganwg, or the Countess of Glamorgan. To add to this status as both a showman and healer, the costumes he wore in public drew the greatest attention to the rather petite Welshman. Dressed in a succession of weird and highly-colourful outfits, the most conspicuous item worn was a fox-skin headress with the tail and legs about his shoulders, hanging as low as his grey hair and beard.

After becoming a father twice by the time he was ninety-three with his unmarried housekeeper who was 60 years his junior, he died sipping a glass of champagne. His own cremation, for which he left full instructions, took place on a hilltop, with 20,000 people assembling to watch the iron coffin set alight. A carnival atmosphere prevailed and the twenty or more pubs in Llantrisant ran dry during the height of the festivities. It is not in his sartorial exploits, pagan amorality or Druidic practices that Dr. Price claims attention in the story of Wales. He is of interest as a true crusading son of rebellion. He understood that showmanship can be helpful to causes. His ringing speeches contain truth to us today but were heresy in his time. He saw the industrial age for what it was, recognised dinginess behind the magnificent Victorian facade, and the mischief wrought by unimaginative and greedy industrialists, to say nothing of the half-educated medical practitioners. He also saw the harm a mishandled religion could do in an uneducated working class population. He claimed that only nature was worth worshipping and man had created God in his own image.

A revolutionary with a zest for living, Dr Price was certainly a majestic figure of high romance who prided himself upon his knowledge of Druidic lore. He longed for the golden age of Wales ruled by the Druids. On moonlit evenings, while grim chapels preached their puritanical doctrine to a congregation groaning in a sense of original sin and while the pits and the ironworks clanged in the new industrial era, Price was high above at the Druid's stones, at one with nature.

He infuriated and frightened, but above all was one of the most brilliant and far-seeing men the nation has ever produced. Despite the passing of time and the growth of the many stories associated with this man, it has become almost impossible to separate fact from fiction as the myth of the doctor grows stronger in the annals of Welsh history. Evidently an eccentric, his behaviour may have bewildered those around him. However, what cannot be denied is the mark he made not only as the prime-mover to legalise cremation but the wonderfully unique role he played in a particularly drab, poverty-stricken Victorian Wales.

Dr William Price was a fascinating, romantic legend and around his name have been woven fantastic tales that will continue to bewilder and delight generations to come.

Chapter One

THE BOY

WILLIAM Price was born in Ty'n-y-coedcae Farm ("the house in the wooded field"), in the parish of Rudry near Caerphilly, Monmouthshire, on March 4, 1800. A clergyman and a few neighbours gathered in the front parlour of the cottage, built sixty years earlier. How could anyone have realised that this baby became the dedicated druid to defy all Christian beliefs, lead a revolutionary movement, be persecuted for his ideals, become visited by feats of fantasy, denounced from the pulpit, have children by women out of wedlock and cremate one of them on a mountaintop?

At that time, the population of South Wales consisted of families who had lived in the area for many generations. With the discovery of coal in the valleys, this would change very soon. At the time, Welsh society appeared to be static, yet it was on the verge of massive change. Educational opportunities were expanding with the work of the Welsh Trust and the Society for the Promotion of Christian Knowledge (the S.P.C.K.). The great breakthrough came with the campaign of Griffith Jones, whose circulating schools were temporary centres providing crash courses in literacy. The establishment of his schools coincided with the early years of the Methodist Revival.

More significant in the long term were economic changes. In the early 18th century, Wales was still an overwhelmingly rural country, although it was gaining an expanding industrial base. Dramatic expansion occurred in the latter 18th century. Although the north-east was the pioneer, the most massive developments occurred in the south-east, where the South Wales coalfield experienced phenomenal growth. Rural Wales also proved volatile, with food riots and enclosure riots. Anti-landlord sentiment developed, especially as the Welsh-speaking, mainly Nonconformist tenantry became increasingly alienated from their English-speaking, Church of England, landlords.

Radical sentiment found expression in the Welsh-language press which began to strike roots in the 1820s. The Welsh, long a conservative people, were coming to embrace the left-wing attitudes which would become characteristic of them in the late 19th and the 20th centuries. Only a few miles from Rudry lay Merthyr Tydfil, once a small village in the upper Taff Valley. The surrounding area contained everything necessary for a successful iron industry - iron ore, limestone for lining furnaces, mountain streams to supply water power, an abundance of timber for the manufacture of charcoal and, if smelting with coke were adopted - ample coal. Ironworks were established at Dowlais in 1749 and at Cyfarthfa in 1765; the former came under the management of the Guest family and the latter under that of the Crawshay family, entrepreneurs of great vigour.

Between 1801 and 1831, the population of Merthyr rose from 7,700 to 46,000, making it the largest town in Wales and the focal point of the source of 40 percent of Britain's iron exports. It led to the massive increase of neighbouring Cardiff, a town with a population of only 1,870 in 1801 and twenty-fifth in size among the towns of Wales. As the port of Merthyr Tydfil, it experienced modest growth over the following three decades. The key development was the opening in 1839 of a large masonry dock, a project conceived and financed by the second Marquis of Bute. In 1841, the dock was linked to Merthyr by the Taff Vale Railway, making it possible for Cardiff to be a major exporter of coal as well as of iron. The superiority of its dock facilities and the rapid growth of coal production in the valleys of the Taff and its tributaries - the Cynon and the Rhondda - enabled Cardiff to capture the bulk of the trade of the South Wales coalfield.

Caerphilly, a town dominated by a sprawling fortress which covered thirty acres of land, making it the largest in Wales, was built in the late 13th century by the Anglo-Norman lord Gilbert de Clare to consolidate his grip on the lands he captured. The village of Rudry was part of the parish of Caerphilly, with just 200 or more inhabitants at the time of Price's birth.

This was the background to a community and a land that would one day hear the name of Dr William Price, either as a great healer or a bizarre eccentric. He was the fifth child of the Reverend William Price (1760-1841) and his wife Mary, an illiterate maid. The reverend, who started life moderately well, was the grandson of Nicholas Pryce, the famed ironmaster from Pentyrch (died November 17, 1757) and owner of the Pentyrch Furnace.

Rev William Price (1760-1841)

7

In 1805, it was taken over by Harford & Partridge and linked with Melin Griffith Works. Nicholas Pryce fathered four sons and two daughters, named Nicholas (of Pontypandy), James, William (also a Pentyrch ironmaster), Charles, Anne (of Pentyrch) and Elizabeth (of Bedwas). His will, dated at Llandaff on February 17, 1758, gives mention to a large estate at Cwm Eldag in Eglwysilan.

The ironmaster's fourth son, Charles Price (1726-1786), who originally settled in Forsett, Redbrook, moved to Bedwas and married Joan Davies (1762-1793) of Gelliwastad, Machen. It was his second marriage. According to a rather unsubstantiated document written by Dr Price in later years, it was said that Joan Davies was a member of the affluent Matthew family, a niece of Admiral Thomas Matthew (1670-1751), who had commanded the Mediterranean Fleet. Apparently, when he was due to retire, he sent a signal to say he would need a house to be built for him.

On his return, when he saw it was a three-storeyed one, he said, "I have lived all my life in a three-decker, and I will not live in it." The house subsequently became the Bishop's Palace at Llandaff and later burned down.

Together, they had four sons. The first was to become the Rev Thomas Price of Merriot. He eventually married Mary Shelland of Somerset and they had four children. The next son was Charles Price, who married Elizabeth Phillips of Monmouth. They had four children and settled in Newport. Rev William Price was the third and Nicholas Price, who died in infancy, was the fourth. The family tree itself is filled with fascinating references to other members of the Price (or Pryce) family.

The greater majority shared the same name — William, Nicholas, Mary, Elizabeth and Ann were particularly commonplace. It is also interesting to note that the majority of the family either settled in Monmouth, Caerphilly, Cardiff or London, except for a cousin, James Price who "died on his passage to Australia."

Rev William Price was born on February 26, 1761 and had three daughters, named Elizabeth (1793-1872), baptised March 23, 1793; Mary (1797-1869), baptised April 13, 1797; and Ann (1804-1878), baptised January 27, 1804. Mary later married Thomas John and settled in Eglwysilan, Pontypridd. It was Elizabeth whom William would later consider a druid like himself.

Two brothers died while still young, the first, William, (baptised August 29, 1795) aged three months.

Elizabeth Price (1793-1872)

Nicholas (baptised January 10 1808) died in 1811 at the age of three as a result of vaccination. The elder son, Charles (1791-1871), baptised in Bedwas on March 16, 1791, was ruinously involved in lawsuits, usually at the instigation of his litigious brother William. He later managed to enjoy a modest life as the cashier to Francis Crawshay, the ironmaster, settling in a property called Primrose Bank in Newbridge (later Pontypridd) with sister Ann.

Rev Price was an ordained priest of the Church of England but never held a living, excusing himself with the plea that he considered it was "too serious an undertaking", although they had some social standing in the locality because there is a family memorial on the north wall of the nave at St Barrwg's Church in Bedwas. His views were strange to say the least and although in later years Dr Price claimed his father was "a druid at heart", which might indeed have been an impediment to his preaching the Gospel, it was a far graver reason that prevented the fulfilment of his priesthood. By the age of thirty, he seems to have been insane.

Psychologists fascinated by the doctor's bizarre behaviour in later life would benefit enormously from a closer inspection of his parentage. Reverend Price was educated at Cowbridge School before being elected a Scholar of Jesus College, Oxford, on February 11, 1780. He voluntarily resigned his scholarship on January 5, 1781, but proceeded to the degree of Bachelor of Arts on June 18, 1783. He was re-elected to his scholarship two months later, becoming a Probationary Fellow on April 6, 1785, after which he took his Master of Arts in April 1786.

He was elected a full Fellow of his college on April 6, 1786 before vacating this under the celibacy rule on May 13, 1790 following his marriage. It was on February 24, 1790, that he married Mary Edmunds of Machen, a maidservant. His wife was considered well below him in station in life, since he was regarded as a pillar of society given his ecclesiastical position, whereas she was just a domestic servant. She could never even sign her own name.

It was, according to Dr Price's own pedigree of the family written in the 1860s, "a most improvident connection in the way of marriage with a woman such below him in station in life, who was in fact only a domestic servant and an unintelligent, illiterate person, and who, though she might have been able to read, was certainly not able to write."

Incidentally, the union was coincidental with some strange behaviour in the young vicar.

Charles Price
(1791-1871)

*Ann Price
(1804-1878)*

In fact, the community of Rudry went so far as to view him as some wild, unruly cleric who took a servant to live in penury in the romantic countryside below the shadow of Caerphilly Castle.

A newspaper report by the infamous Morien of Pontypridd, something of a unreliable source on occasions, written in 1893 following Dr Price's death, said of his father, "He was very eccentric, but not insane according to the usual meaning of the term. A woman of the neighbourhood had once offended him. He saw her going with a basket on her arm in the direction of Caerphilly. Knowing she would return over a footbridge across the Rumney River, he procured a saw and sawed the bridge nearly through. He then waited for the return of his enemy. When he saw her approaching the bridge he called out, 'Take care, you will fall in the river!'. The poor woman, knowing he was not quite right in his head, took no heed of this warning and on reaching the middle of the bridge it gave way under her, and she and the basket fell into the flood. The woman was rescued with no other injury than a wetting."

When discussing his union with Mary Edmunds, the report continues, "This man fell desperately in love with his mother's maid, and they married at Machen Church. Old people, who heard it from their parents, state that when returning home from the church after the wedding, the bridegroom was dancing about the road, and with great glee was shouting, "I have had her - Look! Look!" at the same time pointing her out to the people."

Mary remained with him for the rest of his days and died at the age of 77, on January 5, 1844.

The vicar's arrival at Rudry must have been a great disappointment to the vicar of the parish, who had hoped for an aide from Oxford. Evidences of his insanity appeared more clearly directly after the marriage. For two or three years they were not, apparently, very severe, but were nevertheless evidently the reason he did not follow his career in the church though he was said to have officiated as a clergyman for a while. Rev Price became disheveled in his appearance and engrossed in walks in the woods to collect pieces of bark from the trees in order to burn them piece by piece while muttering uncouth words. Armed with a saw, he became a nuisance to his neighbours as he trespassed on their land to cut wood. He would also collect stones to spit on, which he believed added greatly to their value and put them away carefully.

He also collected snakes, secreting these about his person until he hid them in the stones of the grey tombs of his ancestors. Much to the displeasure of the parishioners, he often carried them in his pocket for days on end.

The reverend had a love of water, bathing in local ponds up to his neck, sometimes fully clothed or only wearing his hat. Occasionally, he bathed naked, but even after he had stripped, he would still drop his clothes in the pond and wear them soaking wet. After his death, he was exhumed so his surgeon-son could rather bizarrely attempt to prove he was *non compos mentis* by showing the vessels of his brain were unduly large. The necropsy examination suggested that the clergyman's desire to immerse himself in water was in order to "relieve the throbbing."

On his death, the bulk of his property was divided between his brother, Rev Thomas Price and his son Charles Price - at least, that was the claim by the young William.

During the trial between Fothergill and Dr Price in later years, it was said that, "more than twenty witnesses were called who had known the unfortunate Rev Price from the time he had been seized with this malady until his death at the age of 76, and they deposed that they never knew him otherwise than a confirmed lunatic, at times a dangerous maniac, at others more tranquil and under control, but at all periods utterly, hopelessly insane; at one time flying through the fields and woods, stark naked, shouting, hollering, bellowing, and again in ragged and torn clothes, carrying bundles of sticks which he would burn, muttering all disjointed sentences. Totally disgusting in his habits and person, frequently dangerous to himself and to others, he presented all the features of the most confirmed debasement of intellect."

On one occasion, he fired off a gun at a young woman who he claimed had been taking sticks from his hedge. He frightened a pregnant woman called Davis so much it allegedly caused the premature birth of her child. On another occasion, he attacked a man by flinging at him a sharp, spear-like weapon which fortunately missed him, but only by inches.

His wife could usually calm him, but often his behaviour would terrify the children so much one of them would be frightened into fits. Or was this simply a case that there was a genetic mental disorder running throughout the children from their lunatic father? There was even the need to call his friends, Owen, Davis and Williams, to restrain him physically, although he never resisted them and would suddenly become incredibly docile.

Arguably, the vicar may well have suffered from a type of schizophrenia, or paraphenia, a condition that was often associated in later life with his son. However, some claimed that the reverend's helpless fits were due to an accident whilst otterhunting. It was recorded that he fell from his horse in 1787 and afterwards the manifestations of his illness presented themselves. Since this was obviously accidental and not a hereditary disease, one cannot assume Dr Price suffered a similar mental disorder. However, living in such an incredibly strange environment must have had a profound effect upon him. Environmentally and genetically, he could not have been born into a more troubled household.

Questions remain unanswered as to whether the reverend was suffering from a genuine mental disorder that had no connection with the alleged accident and therefore could have been inherited by his children, particularly William. In which case, the young William either developed the same strange behavioural pattern because of a genetic disorder, such as paraphenia, or was it simply because he was exposed to such behaviour while a child that it affected him mentally on that level instead? After all, Rev Price's behaviour was somewhat schizophrenic in nature. There was a late onset, after a promising academic career in the church although the personality breakdown was incredibly severe. There's the dress disorder, the running around naked, the violence, the symbolic stones and snakes which all direct towards a deeper mental problem. And yet, the reverend was obviously sane enough to teach his son Latin – this mental illness was obviously sporadic and incredibly peculiar.

His young namesake was the most able member of the Price children. William was baptised in Rudry on April 14, 1800 and following his tenth birthday, and still unable to speak a word of English, he was sent to Mr Gatward's day school at Machen. He walked two miles each day to get there, where he was given instruction on the Lancastrian principle, a system by which the younger children were instructed by the older ones.

Dr Price's father, who would speak only Welsh in the home, sought assistance from an old friend of the family for financial support to send young William to the school, where he learned to speak and read English. Displaying unusual brilliance, despite a disadvantaged background, he passed most of the examination honours before him. His three years of schooling cost £2 8s 0d and at the age of 13, claiming he had absorbed all his master could teach him, he left, despite Mr Gatward's offer of £20 a year salary to stay as an assistant.

Instead, for the next six months, the boy idled away his time, tramping the hills and walking ten or twelve miles a day while reciting Welsh poetry aloud. When he began undressing and exposing his naked body to the sun and wind, he was admonished and threatened by the God-fearing village, but the next day did the same thing. His disgraceful conduct and profitless idleness caused grievance with his parents who urged him to find a living. William hoped to follow a career in medicine, despite his mother's protestations to join the clergy, while his father, who perhaps had something of a surprising insight into the boy's future inclinations, felt he would make a good solicitor. He was accordingly sent to a solicitor's office but William, always the independent son, decided he would become a doctor. He persuaded his father, who was teaching him Latin at home, that he could use this classical knowledge best by being articled to an apothecary. A career in medicine was agreed upon.

Chapter Two

The Student

WHILE Napoleon continued to cause mayhem throughout Europe, in a small town in South Wales William Price became an apprentice to Dr Evan Edwards of Caerphilly. According to a contract, signed on February 21, 1814, William was bound for five years in the sum of £35. The contract made it clear that he was "Not to haunt taverns, inns or ale houses . . . at cards, dice, tables or any other unlawful games he shall not play, nor from the service of his said master day or night shall be absent himself but in all things as an honest and faithful apprentice shall and will behave himself toward his said master."

Evan Edwards was a successful surgeon at the time, for a news report in June 1837 talks of a man called Morgan, a sexton at the 14th century Rudry Church of St James' (where allegedly Oliver Cromwell once took refuge), undergoing an operation for cancer. He had the whole lower lip removed to the chin, then the lower chin brought up to create a new lip. The operation was performed by Dr Edwards and proved a success.

If William served out his time and duty faithfully, he could apply for £20 toward setting himself up in business. The studies proved a great financial strain on the family, and his uncle, Rev Thomas Price of Merriot, Somerset, a son of Jesus College, tried to persuade him to abandon them and return to Gatward's school to take up the position originally offered. The reverend claimed that £20 a year was "more money than many a curate receives after spending hundreds of pounds on his education. You will have five pounds a year advance until you reach the age of 21. You must go, William, and I will get Dr Edwards to liberate you. Why, you will be a man at once!"

William was determined to continue with his studies and Thomas promised to cut off the occasional half-crown gift and would never speak to him again.

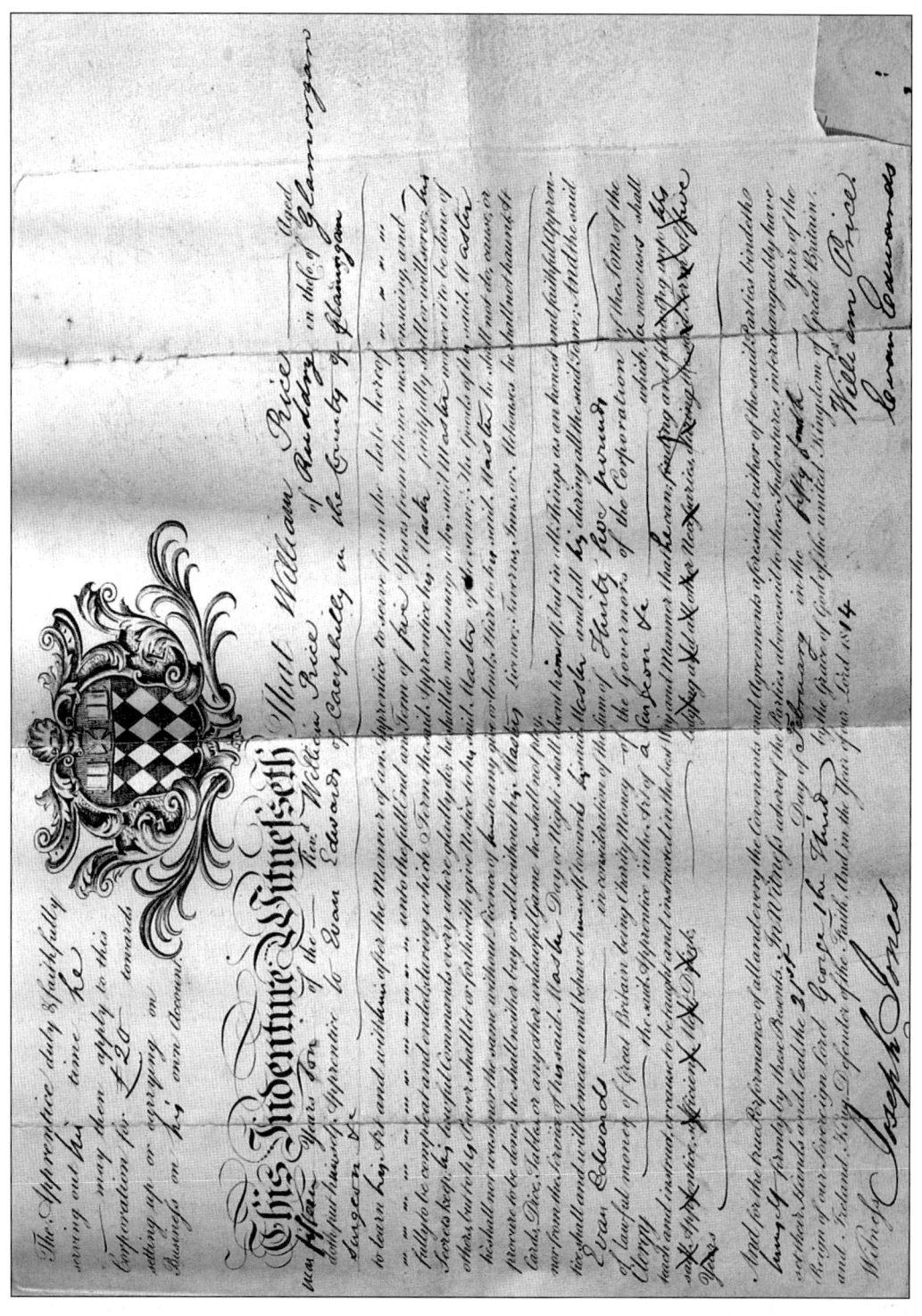

The contract between William Price and Dr Evan Edwards, signed in February 1814.

REPRODUCED BY KIND PERMISSION OF THE MUSEUM OF WELSH LIFE

Obviously, William ignored the threats and continued with his studies. Occasionally, the Corporation of the Sons of the Clergy came to his rescue with small sums to help pay for the tuition and on February 18, 1815, they saw fit to pay Evan Edwards an apprentice fee of £35 less six shillings, being the expense of the indentured.

The document read, "The Corporation of the Sons of the Clergy have been pleased to order an Apprentice Fee of £35 to be allowed for binding *William Price* to you for *five* Years. You therewith receive the Indentures prepared accordingly; the Part having the Receipt endorsed must be executed by you in the Presence of a Witness of Credit, and the Receipt also signed by you in the Presence of the same Witness, and returned to me to remain in the Office of the Corporation. After which the Money will be paid to your Order, by your Bill duly stamped drawn on me payable at Ten Days and not otherwise.

Signed The Registrar, Corporation House, Bloomsbury Place, London."

William, however, was still in a state of poverty and in May 1815 he wrote to his friend, a schoolkeeper called Evans at Ebbw Vale, telling him the situation was extreme and "so much in his shallow pocket as will pay the postage of a letter." It must have seemed to William that his chances of becoming a Licentiate of the Society of Apothecaries were remote.

In 1820, the five-year apprenticeship was over and Price had to produce further certificates of attendance in medical practice at a hospital or dispensary and sit examinations in Latin, pharmaceutical chemistry, materia medica (or pharmacy) and the theory and practice of medicine. Undeterred by poverty, he travelled to London, and it was arranged he should share the lodgings with Daniel Edwards, the brother of Dr Evan Edwards, who lived in Great Trinity Lane, a short walk from Mansion House and St Paul's Cathedral. William probably earned his keep by helping Daniel with his studies in Latin, as he had yet to succeed in becoming a Licentiate of the Society of Apothecaries by the time of Price's arrival in 1820. Daniel had already passed examinations in anatomy and surgery which were required for membership in the Royal College of Surgeons, but the Hall of Apothecaries still eluded him.

In an interview held in 1884 with Ap Idanfryn of the *South Wales Daily News*, Price said, "It was in 1820 I first went to London. I stayed there with Daniel Edwards. He was an excellent fellow, a very humane man, but he was not 'flush' any more than myself. We had to help each other as much as possible.

"He had passed the Royal College of Surgeons, but had not passed through the hall, for he had no knowledge of Latin. We studied hard together. However, I passed through the hall before he was half through his Latin. In fact, I passed the college and the hall in 12 months after I went to London – a thing never done by anyone before me."

The Corporation of the Sons of the Clergy did again come to his aid with the further provision of £20, but this was scarcely enough for his needs. Price was a brilliant student. He entered The London Hospital, Whitechapel, on October 30, 1820 for twelve months under the instruction of Sir William Blizard.

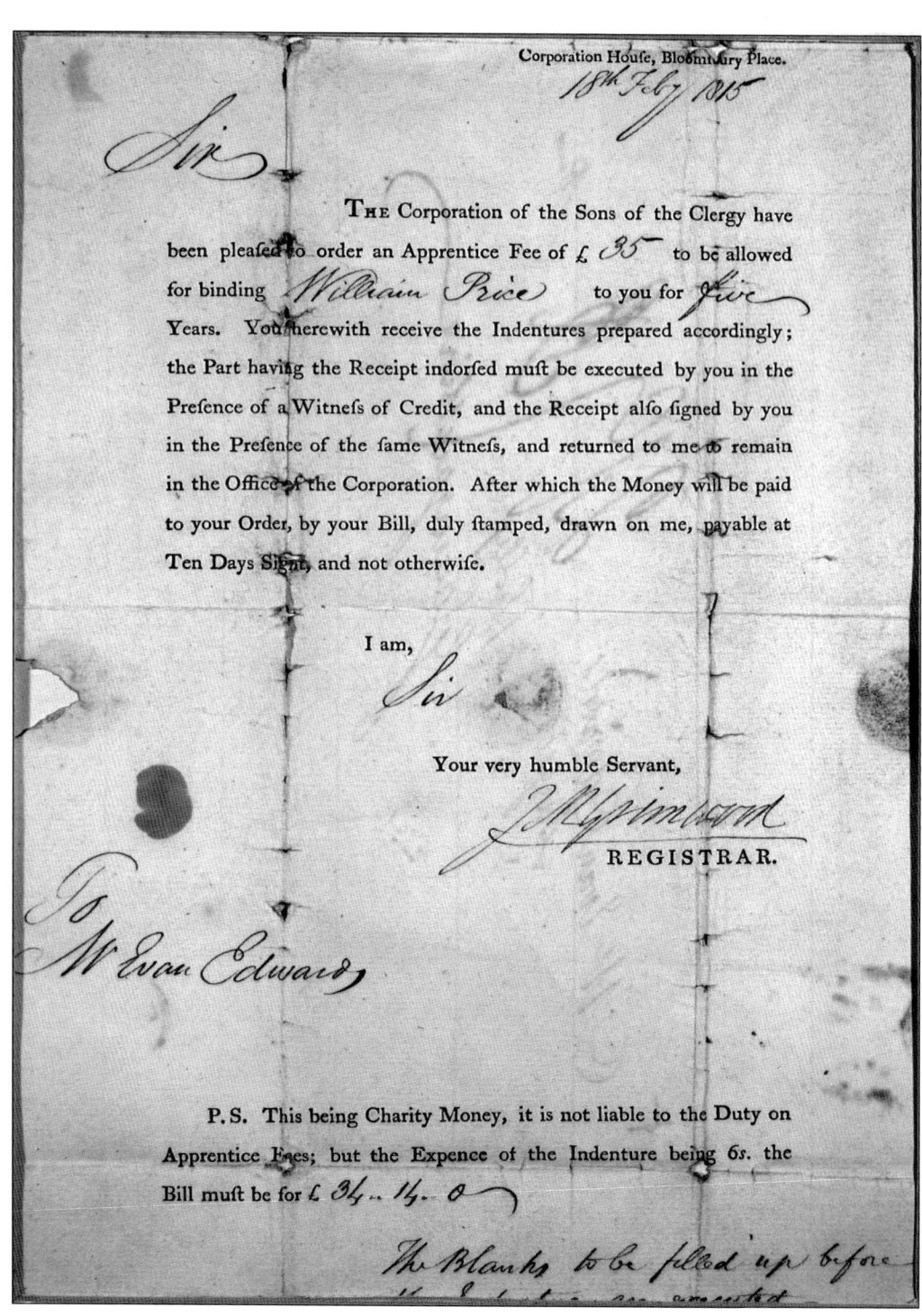

The letter sent to Dr Evan Edwards by the Corporation of the Sons of the Clergy promising to pay £35 for Price's apprenticeship

John Abernethy (1764-1831)

At the same time, he must have registered at St Bartholomew's, a hospital since 1123, under the instruction of John Abernethy. At Barts, there were several hundred surgical students attracted by the reputation of Abernethy - obviously a man after Price's own heart.

Fellow medical student George Hurst wrote: "About the year 1820 I heard with satisfaction the celebrated Abernethy lecture, and his style, manner and simple elocution impressed me greatly. He has been represented as an eccentric, but as a public speaker he was clear, distinct and impressive. By the pupils of the hospital he was esteemed as the highest medical authority of the period, and each student on leaving the hospital considered himself as only second, having received instruction from that great man's discourses."

Short in stature, at five foot six inches high, as was Price, Abernethy was meticulous in dress, manner and mind. His dogmatic, illustrative method of teaching endeared him to his pupils. The son of a merchant from Wolverhampton, he became an apprentice to Sir Charles Blicke at St Bartholomew's in 1779. In 1814, he was appointed Professor of Anatomy and Surgery at the Royal College of Surgeons, and in 1815, after 28 years as assistant surgeon, he became Surgeon to St. Bartholomew's Hospital. By the time young William Price met him, Abernethy was at the peak of his career, running an extensive practice and still an exceptionally popular lecturer. His lectures in anatomy, physiology, surgery, and pathology were considered unequalled. They were, in fact, so popular that they were taken down by fast writers and published in *The Lancet* in 1826 and 1827 - whereupon the publisher was sued by Abernethy.

Although he was a generous man, he deliberately assumed a brusque manner with his patients, assuming it would inspire their confidence. Abernethy lectured in a small amphitheatre, known for its lack of comfort and the stench of the nearby surgical wards adding to the sufferings of the patients and students alike.

One student once observed, "The seats were without rails, and therefore each ascending row of students received the knees of those above in their backs, whilst they thrust theirs into those of the sitters below." Disease could be seen in the wards and methods of post mortems were carried out in public. Often the families wanted to get the body first, while the practitioners wanted to dissect it and it was not uncommon for post mortems to be carried out while the corpse was still warm, causing the blood to gush in abundance.

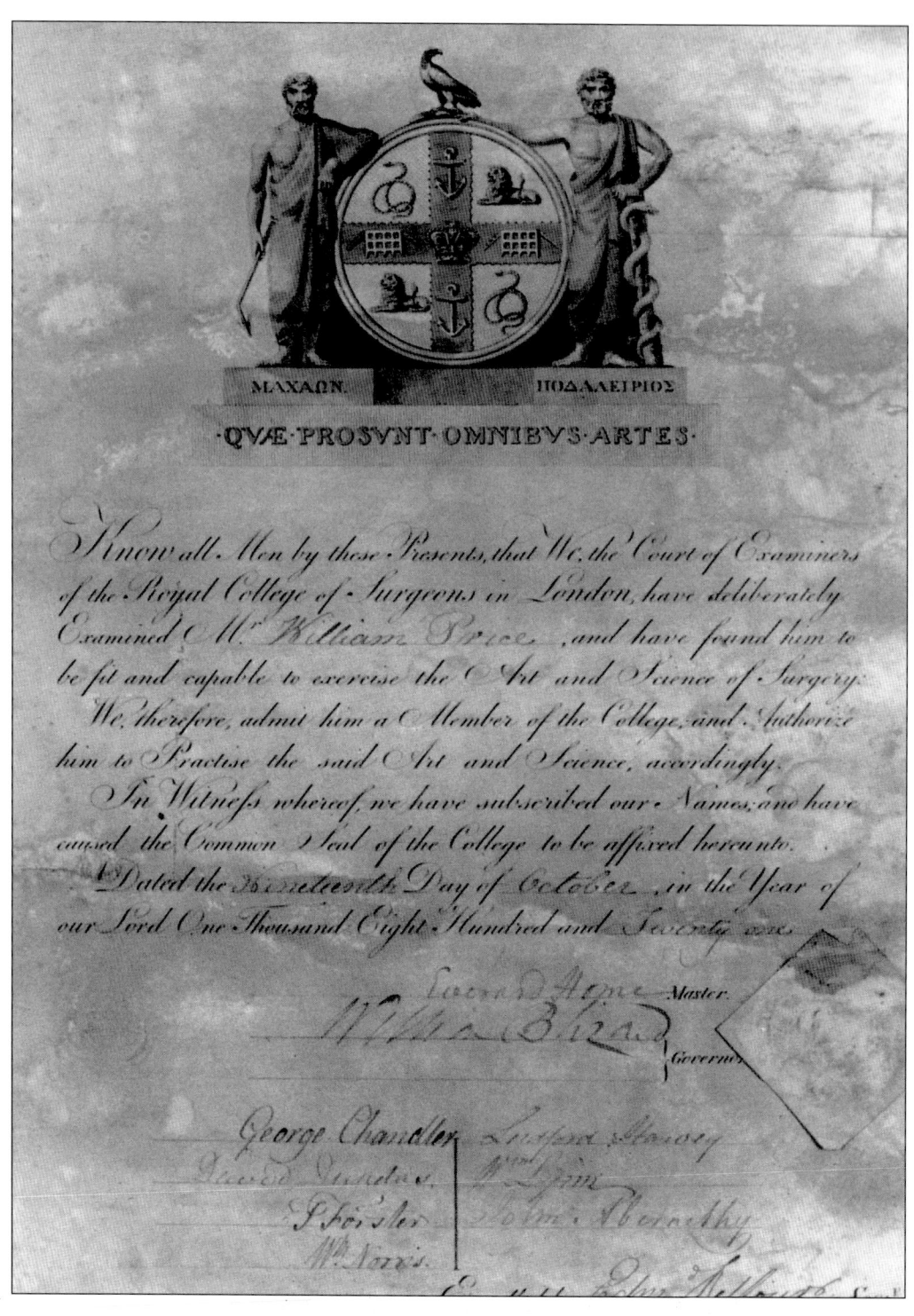

Dr Price's Examination Certificate from the Royal College of Surgeons in London

REPRODUCED BY KIND PERMISSION OF THE MUSEUM OF WELSH LIFE

Abernethy's eccentricities probably influenced Price greatly for the tales told of both master and pupil bear strong resemblance to each other. He was also a man who, like Price, issued wonderful snippets of information to patients which are filled with plain common sense. Typical was the remark to the mother of a girl suffering from stomach complaints: "Why, Madam, do you know there are upward of thirty yards of bowels squeezed underneath that girdle of your daughter's? Go home and cut it; let Nature have fair play, and you will have no need of my advice." One day, Abernethy was visited by a patient complaining of melancholy. "You need amusement," the good doctor declared after a brief examination. "Go and hear the comedian, Grimaldi. He will make you laugh and that will be better for you than any drugs." The patient's reply? "I *am* Grimaldi!"

The young William attended as a surgical dresser for a year during a period in the darkest East End of London when body-snatchers plied their grisly trade to keep up the supply of anatomical dissections. Without doubt, the Welshman was probably more than familiar with the "Resurrectionists" who supplied corpses to his celebrated teacher of anatomy, Dr Edward Grainger. Born in Birmingham in 1797, Grainger had been educated in medicine by his father, and had become a student at the united hospitals of St Thomas's and Guy's in 1816. A dresser to famed surgeon Sir Astley Cooper (1768-1841), he opened an anatomical school at St Saviour's Churchyard, Southwark, three years later, and it proved so successful in rivalling the hospital schools that he built an operating theatre in Webb Street in 1821.

While studying at the hands of such great practitioners, William Price continued to receive letters from his former master, Dr Evan Edwards, who not only continued to show interest in his young apprentice, but apparently began taking his advice on treatment. One letter, written March 16, 1821, read, "I am quite proud to find that you go on so well and be assured that your prosperity at all times will materially add to our comforts. The oil you were kind enough to send me has quite astonished me." William, however, was not yet entitled to the rank of surgeon.

While Price studied under Grainger, the teacher was joined by Dr John Armstrong (1784-1829), a lecturer in the Practice of Physic at the newly opened Webb Street. At first, Amstrong lodged at Great James's Street and published in 1817, "Practical Illustrations of Scarlet Fever, Measles, Pulmonary Consumption and Chronic Diseases, with Remarks on Sulphurous Waters." Fellow medics spoke highly of him; to quote one, "He always spoke from the fullsome of a mind rich in a store of facts which he had collected from his observation of disease. His lectures were attended by many members of the profession, who were powerfully impressed with the originality and boldness of his views."

This was not the case for Price - or at least according to the interview between the druid and Ap Idanfryn when Price was 88 years of age and hardly a reliable source of truth. Price claims that by this time he felt sufficiently confident to instruct Dr John Armstrong on materia medica because he felt the course was deficient.

Price explained, "Dr Armstrong was appointed a lecturer on materia medica at the school but he was as ignorant a man as you could meet.

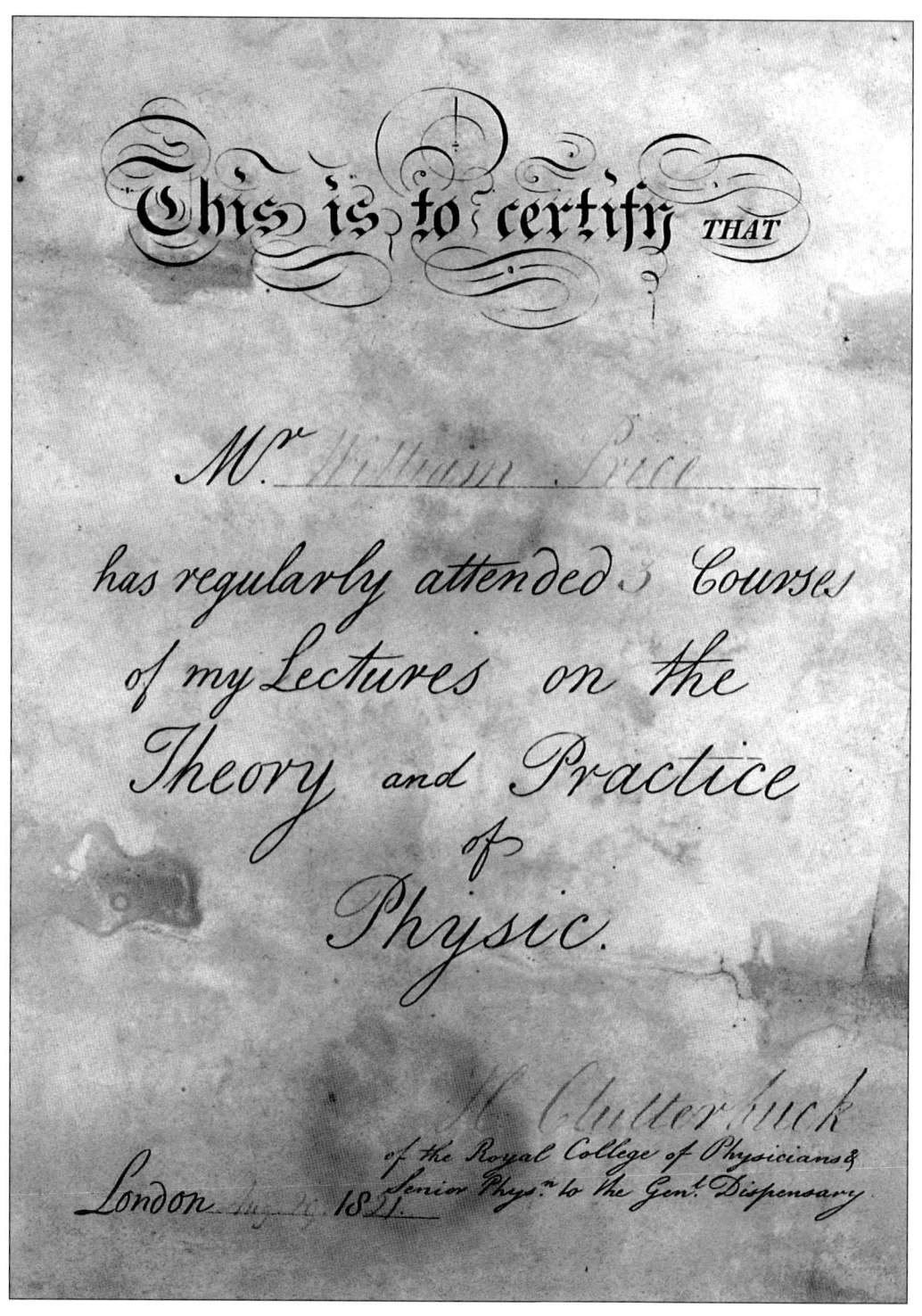

The Certificate certifying that William Price attended lectures on the Theory and Practice of Physics.
REPRODUCED BY KIND PERMISSION OF THE MUSEUM OF WELSH LIFE

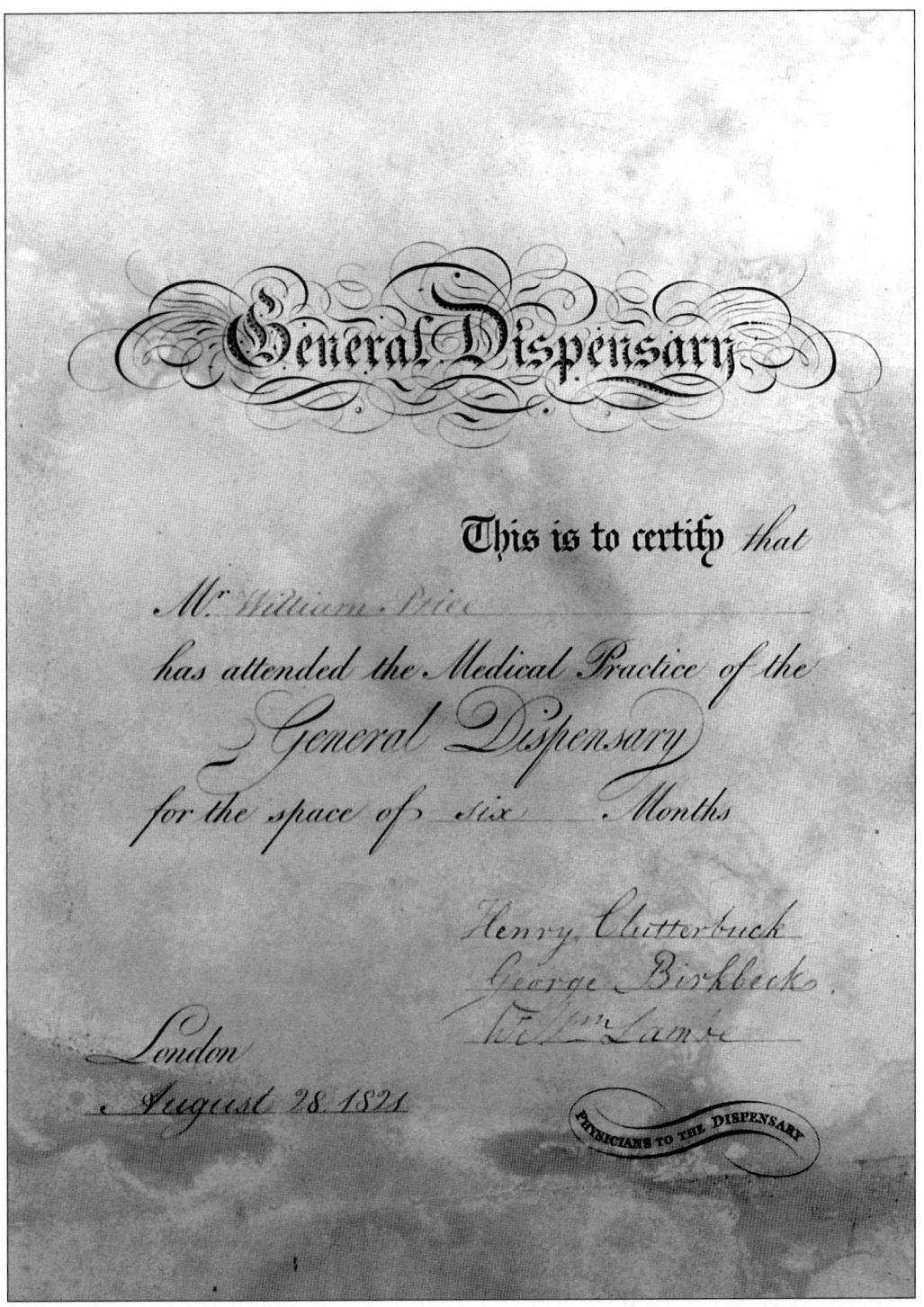

A Certificate showing that Dr Price attended the Medical Practice of the General Dispensary.
REPRODUCED BY KIND PERMISSION OF THE MUSEUM OF WELSH LIFE

William Price, 1822, by Alexander Steward

"He did not know one medicine from another, so he was obliged to put himself under my tuition for four months before he was competent to teach that school, which was attended by more than 400 pupils.

"Oh! I taught him a lot of things – physics, drugs, chemistry – and made him a master of his business. But mind you, this was a secret. It would not do to let the people know that this great man was under the tuition of Dr Price! But he was!

"After that, I got a lot of persons to ground – sometimes I had as many as twenty or thirty at a time. I grounded them all. They call it coaching these days."

Although Price's evaluation of Armstrong seems somewhat harsh, it is interesting to note that the latter had been rejected by the London College of Physicians when he applied for a licence in 1818. Price became a handsome young man about town, with a sufficiently becoming presence to warrant the painting of his portrait by his friend and fellow student, Alexander Steward. In it, he appeared as a young man of proud bearing and penetrating eyes, his thick, black, wavy hair framing a high forehead and his features softened by a kindly mouth. It is faintly inscribed on the back, "This portrait of Mr William Price, member of the Royal College of Surgeons in London, by his friend and fellow student Alexander Steward in grateful thanks for various kindnesses given to him, was presented to his three sisters Elizabeth, Mary and Ann Price July 11, 1822 as a memento which is ever to remind them of the first wish of his heart, namely, that they should always devote the greater part of their leisure to the cultivation of their minds and which they are to retain but on condition of complying with the wish and that of strictly attending to the wishes and suggestions for their improvement of their elder brother Charles Price."

A certificate dated August 28, 1821 confirms he had attended the medical practice of the General Dispensary for six months. Signed by Henry Clutterbuck, George Burberick and William Lambert, Physicians to the Dispensary. Another certificate on the following day certifies he had attended courses in the theory and practice of physic, signed by Clutterbuck of the Royal College of Physicians, Senior Physician to the General Dispensary. On September 6, 1821 William Price was made a Licentiate of the Society of Apothecaries, with a testimonial from Daniel Edwards of Great Trinity Lane. He had attended three lectures and demonstration courses on anatomy and physiology, on the theory and practice of medicine, on chemistry and materia medica and had also spent six months as a probationary practitioner at a general dispensary. A certificate dated September 25, 1821 certifies that Price had attended as a dressing pupil at The London Hospital. This certificate shows a picture of The London Hospital from a 1740 engraving, with the text below reading, "Inasmuch as ye have done it unto the least of one of my brethren ye have done it unto me" (St. Matthew Ch 25 v 40.)

"The London Hospital charitably relieving sick and wounded manufacturers and seamen in merchant service their wives and children. These are to certify that William Price hath diligently attended the practice of surgery as a dressing pupil in this hospital for 12 months. Witness our hand this day September in the year of our Lord 1821 signed William Blizard."

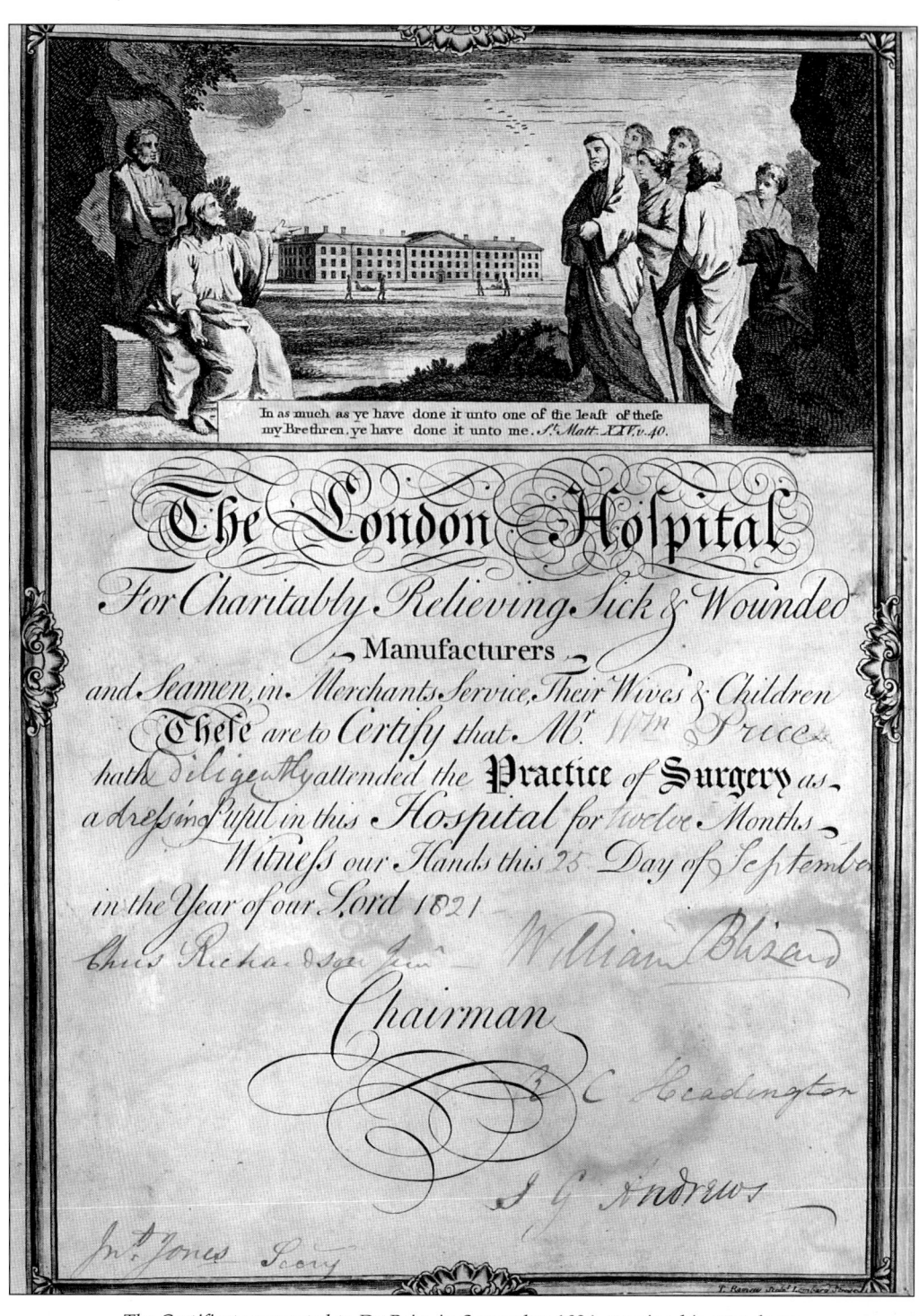

The Certificate presented to Dr Price in September 1821, proving his attendance as a Dressing Pupil at The London Hospital.

REPRODUCED BY KIND PERMISSION OF THE MUSEUM OF WELSH LIFE

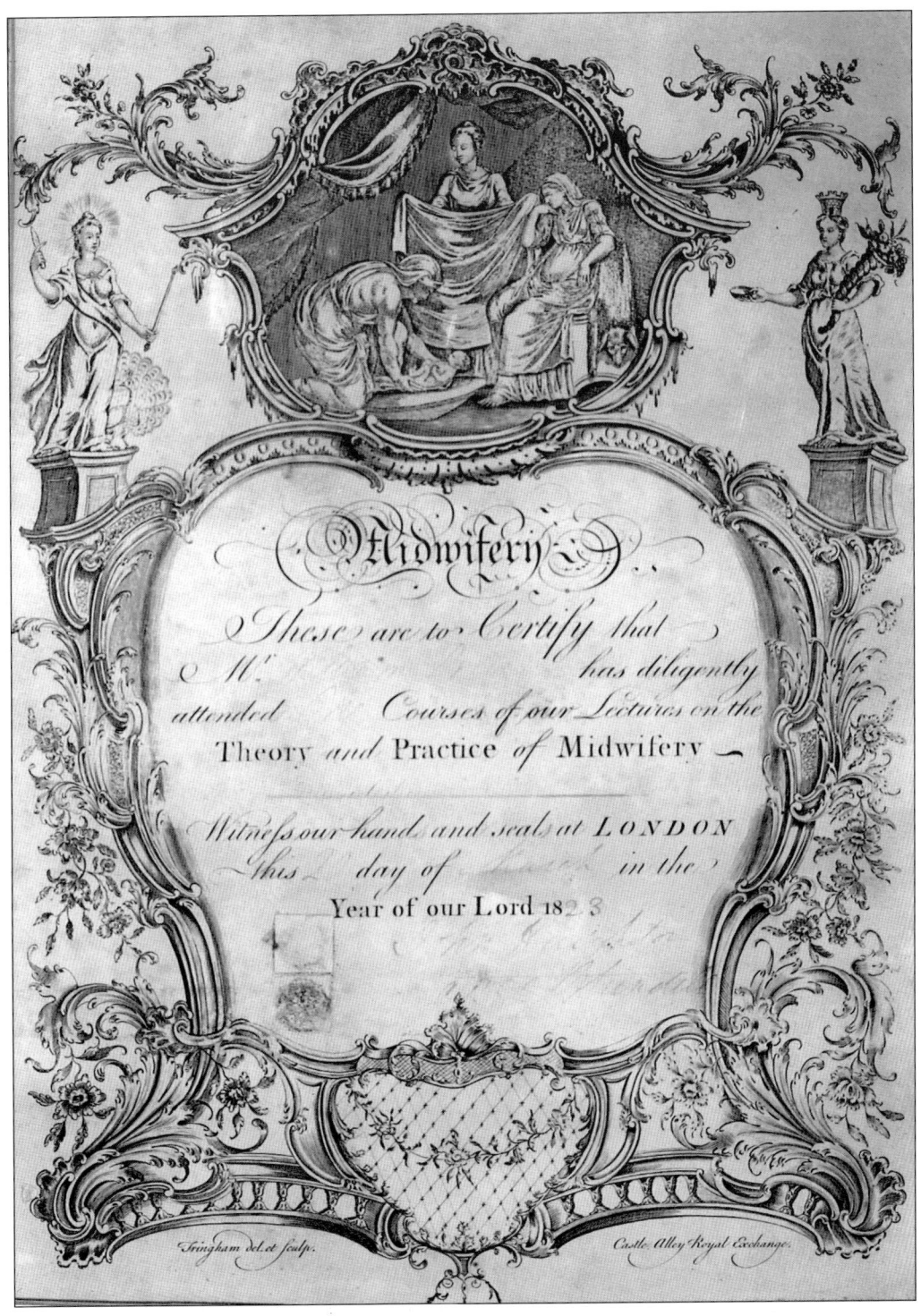

The Certificate confirming William Price's attendance in lectures on Midwifery.

REPRODUCED BY KIND PERMISSION OF THE MUSEUM OF WELSH LIFE

On October 19, 1821, he was made a member of the Royal College of Surgeons in a certificate signed by Sir William Blizard, John Abernethy and others. At the age of 21, he was a well-qualified young man. Despite his attainment, he continued to study, and that winter attended a further three courses on lectures on anatomy and physiology, under his old teacher, Edward Grainger. He also dissected during the same period. The fee was £20 and the cost for the Licentiate of the Society of Apothecaries was somewhere in the region of £3.10s.

At this time, Price worked for a notable Scottish gentleman named John Forbes, possibly the same Forbes who was a merchant in Bombay. There are references made to a Forbes (1743-1821), better known as Bombay Jock, who founded the family fortune that led to the erection of Castle Newe in Aberdeenshire. It seems perfectly possible, since the Forbes referred to in Dr Price's life was a man who had been in India and ruined his constitution in a warm climate. He called on Price to care for him and allegedly pleaded with the young doctor to stay with him until he died. For the last ten months of his life, Price nursed the patient at his London home.

By now, London had no more to offer him and he considered travelling to India, but his cousin, Dr Charles Price of Brighton (son of his reverend uncle), advised him to return to Wales. As much as £500 was needed to secure an apprenticeship to a leading surgeon. The physicians were a very select body whose circle Price had not penetrated; it was exceptional for anyone to gain election to their fellowship unless they were a graduate of Oxford or Cambridge. The snobbery in the higher ranks of the medical world left a bitter taste in the young doctor's mouth. However, his new qualifications fitted him well for general practice in Wales. It was time to go home.

Chapter Three

THE SURGEON

AT first, Dr Price returned to his family home at Rudry, Caerphilly, later moving to the rather grand address of Ynys y Llewod Duon (River Isle of the Black Lions), somewhere between Tongwynlais and Pentyrch. He probably worked for some time as a surgeon to the Pentyrch Works, once owned by his great-grandfather.

From there he moved to Nantgarw eventually opening a surgery at Craig yr Helfa, Glyntaff, where his talents were sufficient for him to be in constant demand. According to Price, he remained there for seven years, later setting up home at Porth y Glo Farm in Upper Boat, rented from the father of a solicitor from Cardiff. He filled the farm with goats and cattle, some of which he named Gertrude, Price and Jenner.

Craig yr Helfa Surgery, Glyntaff

According to a newspaper report by Morien in 1893, "The goats inflicted great injury to every green tree on the farm and in the neighbourhood.

"After he had been there some time, Mr Grover, the solicitor, gave him notice to leave, but Dr Price would not go".

Y Maen Chwyf (The Rocking Stone), Pontypridd

"An action of ejectment was instituted, and, in the midst of intense popular excitement, his goats and cattle were turned out into the highway. Dr Price himself had retired into the farthest room in the house. He was carried out sitting on a chair, and placed on the road."

In June 1823, he was appointed medical adviser to the Crawshay family, the wealthy ironmasters of Merthyr and Treforest. He became the chief surgeon – following an election by the workforce - for the Brown Lenox Chainworks (Ynysangharad Works) in Newbridge or Pontypridd and remained in the post for almost fifty years, until 1871. It was the only time known in British history for the workforce to elect their own medical officer. Opened in 1818, the works made Pontypridd the unlikely centre of manufacture of chain cable and anchors for warships and merchant vessels.

It seems rather ironic that he should work so closely with the Crawshays, particularly owing to his open denunciation of ironmasters and coal mine owners generally. During this time, he engaged in general practice and felt sufficiently well established to build a house opposite Pentyrch works, the first of a number of projects that were never completed.

He described the problems associated with the scheme in his 1888 interview with Ap Idanfryn, "I began to build a house for myself opposite Pentyrch. Mr Blakemore, the owner of the site, had promised me a lease for 99 years, but he wanted me to do something there against my will and I refused. 'Very well', he said, 'I will not give you a lease on the place and I will not return you a shilling of the money you have spent there'.

"I had spent over £200 and the lodge is there now. So I put him in Chancery and got my money back. My brother, who was in Blakemore's employment as a clerk at the tin works, was very angry with me for this.

"I went to my brother's house at Pentyrch but he tried to throw me out. He was four or five inches taller than I, but I was stronger, so I soon put him on his back and gave him a good licking. He got notice to leave the works, but as I was a great friend of Crawshay, I got a place for him at Cyfarthfa Works and he remained there for 16 years."

His practice in Glyntaff was a place not so far from Pontypridd Common at Coedpenmaen, where the effects of "Druidomania" were renowned. It was these Neo-Druidic rites taking place on the famous Rocking Stone (Y Maen Chwyf) that undoubtedly drew Price into a circle of fellow druids. Fantastically dressed and chanting a "Song of the Primitive Bard to the Moon", he often performed his sacred messages there in later years as a few disciples clustered around the authoritative and impressive doctor who held a crescent-topped staff high in the air.

Pontypridd (known as Newbridge until 1856), in the early Victorian era showed tremendous growth. Situated at the point at which the two Rhondda Valleys and the Taff Valley meet, it was one of the fastest-growing towns in Wales.

Newbridge Works (Brown Lenox) c.1840

A canalside hamlet, it was famous for its 18th-century bridge, built in 1756 by William Edwards. It was the third attempted by Edwards, and at the time of construction was the longest stone-built, single-arch bridge in Europe. The history of Pontypridd is closely tied to the coal and iron industries. It later became an important location for the transportation of coal from the Rhondda, and iron from Merthyr Tydfil, first via the Glamorganshire Canal and later via the Taff Vale Railway to the ports at Cardiff and Barry.

As Price established himself as a leading local practitioner, the dawning of the Victorian era was about to begin. Her reign brought impressive events such as the Great Exhibition at the Crystal Palace to display industrial and scientific progress. It saw the introduction of the penny post, crinoline fashions and the Charge of the Light Brigade. As the British "scrambled" for Africa, Stanley raised his hat to greet Dr Livingstone, he presumed. Her Majesty celebrated a life surrounded by important writers, poets, architects, artists and musicians. Filled with pomp and circumstance, this was the era of the railway, of Brunel and the feats of engineers. In Wales, it was a new era, too, and Price's ideals and behaviour hardly made him the model of Victorian propriety. Far from it, in fact.

Wales was undergoing a rapid social transformation in the 19th century. It opened with major incidents of risings and riots. In Merthyr, Newport and later the Rebecca Riots of West Wales, the Welsh were taking matters into their own hands. It comes as little surprise why the outcome of a government inspection into the Welsh people in 1847 was the greatest insult this country had ever received. The 1,200 page Blue Books inspection portrayed the Welsh as ignorant, drunken, immoral, dirty and uncivilised. It was a devastating attack across Wales and the people were outraged and also ashamed by the outcome.

Once more, they felt inferior to their English neighbours and from this sense of shame were determined to show themselves as model Victorians. They succeeded, of course, suddenly displaying themselves as respectable and loyal citizens of the throne. Although they failed to succeed in curbing the drinking habits of the working miner, there was a major facet of Welsh life which created a purer image of its people – nonconformism. Chapel life was central to a community, as the hub of more than just religion. Aside from chapel services, there were benefits of a busy social life, too, in society meetings, Bands of Hope, gymanfa ganu, political debate and, of course, choralism.

The latter inflamed passions like tribal warfare, creating an entire, new, universal image of Wales as the "land of song". It showed the Welsh were as good, if not better, than the rest of the world and saw them receive the royal seal of approval with a massed mixed choir performing for the Queen at Crystal Palace in 1872. This sense of respectability, or order, of religion, of loyalty to the throne, the very ideals of a Victorian society, must have infuriated Dr Price, the young radical.

His work was based in Treforest, a revolutionary town, far ahead of neighbouring Newbridge. It was the hub of industry and one of the capitals of the Crawshays. The family, originally from Yorkshire, were the owners of a vast iron empire.

*Francis Crawshay
(1811-1878)*

Richard Crawshay (1739-1810) had initially leased, and then purchased, the ironworks of Anthony Bacon at Cyfarthfa in Merthyr Tydfil, which prospered over a short period of time. On his death in 1810, Crawshay bequeathed three-eighths of his property to his son William, three-eighths to his son-in-law Benjamin Hall and two-eighths to his nephew Joseph Bailey. The Cyfarthfa works were carried on by William, who in 1825 built Cyfarthfa Castle at a cost of £30,000.

William (1788-1867) acquired the old Hirwaun Works and Collieries for his sons Henry and Francis, who succeeded him after his death. He soon lost interest in Treforest and its tinplate works, delegating the completion of the modernising process of the project to Francis (1811-1878), who allegedly fathered 24 illegitimate children and named streets in the town after them. While living in Forest House, Francis sold the entire works to a consortium which set up the Treforest Iron and Steel Company. He was popular with his millhands and seems to have had a kind streak in him and a genuine interest in the welfare of his men and their families. He was the man with whom Dr Price was closely associated and when studying the industrialist, it becomes obvious why. Ironically, he built the first "Round House" at Rhydyfelin in 1850. It is said they were built in this circular design to stop housewives gossiping on the doorsteps. Others say Francis had a bet with his brother over who could build eight houses on the smallest piece of land. Whatever the reason, the Round House design was later adopted by Dr Price for his project at Glyntaff.

In the early 1830s, when Francis was put in charge of Hirwaun Ironworks, and a new tinplate works at Treforest, he was regarded as a somewhat eccentric character. Refusing to reside at the family home of Ty Mawr, Hirwaun, he preferred instead to live at a cottage to the north of the works. He was known as 'Mr Frank' by the workers and learned to speak Welsh in order to communicate with them.

Francis later moved to Treforest, where he lived at Forest House, the heart of a university built there more than a century later, with his wife and eight legitimate children. It was during this time that he became friends with Dr Price. Francis himself erected his own Druidic circle at Forest House, which was eventually demolished during the 1950s in order to provide space for the expanding School of Mines. He was particularly fond of the sea and owned a steam yacht in which he often sailed to France. His heart was never in his work and he preferred shooting rabbits on Barry Island, which he owned.

The Druidic circle at Forest House, Treforest, erected by Francis Crawshay

Following the closure of the Hirwaun and Treforest works in 1859 and 1867 respectively, Francis retired to Bradbourne Hall, Sevenoaks, where it was said he enjoyed walking around in nautical dress.

Professor Meic Stephens explained, "Having many illegitimate offspring in Treforest, Francis held parties and balls at the House. Following retirement, he lived out his years in Kent, striking church bells which he put up in the grounds of his home much to the annoyance of the villagers. Along with his brother Henry, they erected a number of neo-Egyptian obelisks in the village, replicas of the one erected at Heliopolis by Osonseen, the first Pharaoh."

Yet again, eccentric behaviour seems to ring aloud with Francis Crawshay and it seems little wonder why he became a close ally of Dr Price. Egyptian and, most of all, Greek history was a love of Price's also, along with an interest in Hindu literature and creeds. It is said the bond between Price and Crawshay came about after the doctor had saved the life of the ironmaster's wife in 1842 by successfully delivering her of a child by Caesarean section birth – possibly on the kitchen table. This tale, like so many in Price's life, was never confirmed. Although the godless Crawshay paid for the building of several chapels in the districts, he was at heart a pagan who was sympathetic towards the heresies of Dr Price. While discussing the subject in later life, and at a time when his mind was hardly as lucid, Dr Price explained, "I believe in nothing except what I know to be absolutely in existence. I use the Bible as it ought to be used. It is clear to me that Abraham was a cannibal, and it was the view of destroying that trait in the nature of his descendants, and to raise tame animals, that the first pyramid in Egypt was built."

Price hated the gloomy religion of the chapels and despised sanctimonious preachers, who he said only led people at funerals. He felt religion had been used to enslave, claiming, "Man is greater than God. For Man created God in his own image". The only thing to worship in his life was nature itself. He once said, "Preachers are paid to teach that the world of thieves and oppressors, of landlords and landowners, is a just world. Their theology is the doctrine that the powers that be are ordained by God."

Dr Price considered the Rocking Stone at Pontypridd to be a primitive Druidic temple. It was regarded as a sacred altar for the Druids and is of local pennant stone that may have been deposited on the Common as a result of a glacial action, in which case making it older as a Druidic settlement than Stonehenge. The stone is balanced on a natural rock base and weighs about nine tons, which once could have rocked easily. Claiming to be steeped in Druidic lore, his love of this part of Wales was blatant.

The Druidism of Pontypridd is of early 19th century creation. Arch-forger Iolo Morganwg, the Archdruid of Wales, is said to have presided over a ceremony held there in 1815 and at several others subsequently.

Born Edward Williams in Llancarfan in March 1747, he later lived in Cowbridge, and used his bardic name throughout his long life. A renowned forger and collector of medieval Welsh documents, he is recognised as the godfather of the neo-Druidism phenomenon. He claimed to have manuscripts which proved that Druidism and the bardic tradition had continued unmolested in Glamorgan since the days before the Romans, through the introduction of Christianity, and into the modern era. He was, of course, wrong. Morganwg had the fear that the Welsh were losing their heritage and traditions, and so felt he had to preserve and reintroduce them to the public. Unfortunately, some of this task involved forging documents and creating traditions.

Iolo Morganwg (1747-1826)

He moved to London in 1770, and quickly took to meso-Druidism, which had been flourishing for 75 years. Always in bad health, he moved back to Glamorgan and in 1792 created Gorsedd Beirdd Ynys Prydain, an assembly of Welsh poets, which merged with the Eisteddfod and continues to this day. His literary career spanned from 1770 to 1826, during which time he adapted the ideas of romanticism that were sweeping across Europe, for the benefit of his own people by providing them with lyrical poetry and romantic history. In assessing his career, it is difficult to know the effect his addiction to laudanum may have had on him. Irritable, a case-hardened romancer, an inveterate fabulist, hypochondriac and fabricator, he was also the finest scholar of his time in Wales.

Professor Meic Stephens explained: "For Iolo, Wales had been the last bastion of the Druids before they were annihilated by the Romans in AD 61 and, in his book, *Cyfrinach Beirdd Ynys Prydain*, Glamorgan was presented as being at the heart of the Welsh literary tradition.

"To prove his thesis, he fabricated a large number of fine poems and other texts. These he attributed either to Dafydd ap Gwilym, the greatest Welsh poet of the medieval period, or to Glamorgan poets who had never existed. He even composed illustrious biographies for some of them. The Gorsedd ceremonies proved popular and in 1858 became part of the pageantry of the National Eisteddfod. There, every August, they continue to lend colour to the affairs of a people who have been rather starved of indigenous ritual.

"After Iolo's death, his son Taliesin Williams (1787-1847), a schoolmaster in Merthyr, propagated his father's work among the poets of the Blaenau. The best that can be said for Neo-Druidism is that it was the dream of men who refused to accept the recorded view of the history of their country and who refurbished the past by inventing traditions which mirrored their own aspirations. They sought refuge in the Wales of their imaginations at a time when understanding their country's history, language and literature had long been neglected.

"Among a dispossessed people, the main objective was not so much to demonstrate the intrinsic qualities of the Welsh language and its literature, as to show that the Welsh people had an honourable place in the British scheme of things – indeed, that they alone should be considered the true Britons. Iolo's claims for his native and beloved Glamorgan found fertile ground in the minds of Newbridge (Pontypridd) men, and his influence lingered in the district for long after his death in 1826."

Iolo's son, Taliesin ab Iolo Morganwg, presided over a Gorsedd at the Rocking Stone in September 1834. The Druids afterwards retired to the house of fellow Druid Gwilym Morganwg, which formed part of the New Inn Hotel on Taff Street, where the bard was landlord at the time.

A serpent of standing stones surrounds the Rocking Stone. It is made up of two concentric circles, joined to a winding avenue of stones, ending in a small circle that has the two eyes of the serpent. It is believed that Evan Davies (1801-1888), a clockmaker, created the serpent in 1850. Known as Myfyr Morganwg (The Student of Glamorgan), he settled in Pontypridd in 1844 and, according to Morien, "He was universally known as the Archdruid, having succeeded Taliesin ap Iolo Morganwg to that dignity in 1847."

Myfyr was born on January 6, 1801 in a farmhouse just north-west of Pencoed. Having received no formal education, he devoted himself in his youth to the mastery of the Welsh bardic rules and the study of mathematics. At first, he called himself Ieuan Myfyr and began to preach in congregational chapels near his home. He came into prominence in 1842 by debating on the subject of temperance, in a public meeting held in Llantrisant. The discussion was between himself and the eccentric Rev John Jones of Llangollen. The subject "Was alcoholic drink prohibited in the Bible?" saw Myfyr dismiss the claim. At the time, thousands turned out for the public debate given the fact that temperance was such a major subject throughout South Wales.

Settling in Mill Street, Pontypridd, he came deeply under the influence of the Druidic "fever" sweeping the market town. Reading books on the religions of the East, he believed Christianity was Druidism in a Jewish garb.

Myfyr won the chair at the Pontypridd Eisteddfod in 1854 for the Welsh ode *The Sacred Circles of the Bards* and held Druidic ceremonies at the Rocking Stone until 1878. These meetings were held at the time of the equinoxes and the two solstices. He published several books dealing with Druidism and was appointed to adjudicate essays on the Madogwys – the descendants of Madoc who had allegedly discovered America centuries before Christopher Columbus reached the West Indies – in the Llangollen Eisteddfod of 1858. He appeared at the event wearing a "Druidical Egg" on his chest.

He died in Pontypridd on February 23, 1888 and was buried with copies of his publications placed under his head.

Myfyr Morganwg (1801-1888)

His grave, also occupied by his wife Sarah, was a few yards on the right-hand from the entrance into Glyntaf churchyard. Like Morien, his fellow Druid, he had enjoyed a long association with Price, although it seems as if the group didn't always agree on the same Druidic beliefs.

Price disputed the title of Archdruid of Wales with Myfyr, claiming only he had the key to the secrets of the Druids. Professor Stephens explained: "Myfyr claimed to have discovered the secret of earthly wisdom, which he kept in the shell of an ostrich's egg slung round his neck on a piece of string.

"In short, he believed that Christianity was but a Semitic form of Druidism, a fantastic theory which he expounded in such books as *Gogoniant Hynafol y Cymry (The Ancient Splendour of the Welsh)*, published at Pontypridd in 1865.

"Some thought his Druidomania had been caused by his failure to be appointed minister of the Independent chapel known as Sardis, one of the largest in the town. Be that as it may, by 1847, together with Taliesin Williams, Myfyr was claiming to be the true Archdruid of Wales.

"This was a delusion which, for the next 40 years, at solstice and equinox, he acted out in quasi-religious ceremonies from the Rocking Stone, much to the consternation of the more orthodox of the townspeople. For all his outlandish beliefs and behaviour, there was no doubting his sincerity.

"Myfyr was one of a circle of poets known as Clic y Bont ("The Bridge Clique"). Besides Myfyr, there was Dewi Haran (David Evans, 1812-85); Dewi Wyn O Essyllt (Thomas Essile Davies, 1820-91); Camelian (Cosleff Cosleff, 1834-1910); Glanffrwd (William Thomas, 1843-90); and Brynfab (Thomas Williams, 1848-1927), to mention only a few of the clique's leading members, and were all men of some substance and not without literary ability.

"They gave Pontypridd a literary identity at a time when the town was beginning to need one. Pontypridd was still only a random assembly of industrial undertakings of one sort or another.

"It consisted of hastily thrown up and insanitary houses, deemed good enough by the coalowners and ironmasters for workers and their families to live in, and it was a place where local government was still embryonic and politics still at a semi-feudal stage of development. Still, the town was nevertheless the meeting place of this small group of writers who met regularly to discuss and practise their craft."

It was in this "frontier" town of Pontypridd, surrounded by fellow "Druids" and individuals, that Price flourished as both a local surgeon and philanthropist. He was already an active participant in the eisteddfodau held by the Cymreigyddion Society of Newbridge and in 1837, the year Victoria became Queen, he offered £10 in prizes at a local eisteddfod - £1 each for the best essay on the subjects of Love, Pride, Belief, Faith, Superstition, Prejudice, Fame, Opinion, Profit and Truth.

All proceeds would go towards the creation of a centre of culture in Pontypridd. In the following year, Price issued a public appeal for funds to preserve the monumental relics of the Rocking Stone by the erection around them of a tower 100ft high at a cost of £1,000.

A document printed on March 7, 1838 by W. Bird of Cardiff, on behalf of Dr Price, was entitled "Y Maen Chwyf" and made fascinating reading: "My lords, ladies and gentlemen! I beg to call your attention, and all those who feel interested in the Preservation of the Ancient Institutions and Antiquities of Britain, and especially to this PRIMITIVE TEMPLE, "Y MAEN CHWYF". This Druidic Temple is situated on Coedpenmaen Common, on the left of the Taff near Ponty y Ty Perydd, on the verge of the precipice, a little north-east of Ynysangharad Works.

"In the immediate vicinity of this temple, the graves of the aborigines occupy a space of about 40,000 square yards. While the population of this neighbourhood continued to follow agriculture, Y Maen Chwyf was in no danger of being injured, as the hereditary veneration which descended from father to son, through successive generations, was sufficient to shield it from rude hands. But it is not so now.

"The legions of artificers, manufacturers and strangers that advance on this place from all directions have no idea of reverence for this beautiful temple. Hence, it is that some few years ago an attempt was made to destroy it. Mr Thomas of Ynysangharad heard of it just in time to save it from ruin.

"From this brief history, then, it appears that it requires no great genius to foretell the fate that awaits this most ancient monument.

Y MAEN CHWYF.

My Lords, Ladies, and Gentlemen!

I BEG to call your attention, and all those who may feel interested in the Preservation of the Antient Institutions and Antiquities of Britain, and ESPECIALLY to this PRIMITIVE TEMPLE, "Y MAEN CHWYF." This Druidic Temple is situate on COEDPENMAEN COMMON, on the left bank of the Taff, near Pont y Ty Perydd, on the verge of the precipice, a little north-east of Ynysyngharad Works.

In the immediate vicinity of this temple, the graves of the aborigines occupy a space of about 40,000 square yards.

While the population of this neighbourhood continued to follow agriculture, Y Maen Chwyf was in no great danger of being injured, as the hereditary veneration which descended from father to son, through successive generations, was sufficient to shield it from *rude* hands. *But it is not so now.*

The legions of artificers, manufacturers, and strangers, that advance on this place from all directions, have no idea of reverence for this beautiful temple.

Hence it is that some few years ago an attempt was made to destroy it. Mr. Thomas, of Ynysyngharad, heard of it just in time to save it from ruin.

From this brief history, then, it appears that it requires no great genius to foretel the fate that awaits this most antient monument.

Under this impression, it was suggested to "Cymdeithas y Maen Chwyf," that a Tower of one hundred feet high be built by public subscription near Y Maen Chwyf; the space within the Tower to be divided into eight apartments for a Museum, and surmounted with a Camera Obscura. This Tower will command a horizon of ten miles radius. And that a spacious house, some distace from Y Maen Chwyf, be built for the Bard of the Society to reside in, to take care of the temple.

This proposition has been unanimously seconded by the Society and the whole neighbourhood, as will be seen by the subscribers' names, *in the order given*.

The estimated cost of these erections is £1000. The revenue of the Tower will be about £100. per annum. With the greater part of this sum the Society will establish a Free School, to be kept by the Bard of the Society, for educating the children of the poor. The remainder will go to defray the expenses of the institution In this way, Y Maen Chwyf will not only be preserved, but will continue to operate as a mighty engine of civilization, the Nucleus of a Museum, the parent of the tower that is destined to protect it, and to dispense the blessings of education to the industrious classes of the community.

Y MAEN CHWYF will represent the seed, the tower, the tree, and the inimitable landscape of the Camera Obscura, the fruit of knowledge. A question has been asked us, *will* the brinker landlords—viz., Lord Dynevor, B. Hall, Esq., M.P., J. Bassett, Esq., Mrs. Morgan, the Hon. R. H. Clive, and the Marquess of Bute, permit the Bards to protect and preserve their temple? Our answer has been and is, WE HAVE NO DOUBT they will not only charter our prescriptive right to protect the Druid's temple, but express their sense of approbation by directing their names to be added to the list of subscribers for its preservation,—

"One common cause makes millions of one breast,
Slaves of the East, or Helots of the West;
On Andes' or on Athos' peaks unfurll'd,
The self-same standard streams o'er either world."

As some may question the applicability of the word Temple, at the present day, to designate an immense rude and *poised* fragment of Rock, on an elevated plain, with no other covering than that of the sky, I beg leave most humbly to submit, that it is infinitely more deserving of that term, than the Temple of Jupiter Ammon, in Thebes. As none will dispute, I think,

Y Maen Chwyf, published by Dr Price in March 1838.

"Under this impression, it was suggested to Cymdeithas y Maen Chwyf", that a Tower of one hundred feet high be built by public subscription near Y Maen Chwyf; the space within the Tower to be divided into eight apartments for a Museum, and surmounted with a Camera Obscura. This Tower will command a horizon of ten miles radius. And that a spacious house, some distance from Y Maen Chwyf, be built for the Bard of the Society to reside in, to take care of the temple.

"This proposition has been unanimously seconded by the Society and the whole neighbourhood, as will be seen by the subscribers' names, in the order given. The estimated cost of these erections is £1000. The revenue of the Tower will be about £100 per annum. With the greater part of this sum, the Society will establish a Free School, to be kept by the Bard of the Society for educating the children of the poor. The remainder will go to defray the expenses of the institution.

"In this way, Y Maen Chwyf will not only be preserved, but will continue to operate as a mighty engine of civilisation, the nucleus of a museum, the parent of the tower that is destined to protect it, and to dispense the blessings of education to the industrious classes of the community.

"Y MAEN CHWYF will represent the seed, the tower, the tree, and the inimitable landscape of the Camera Obscura, the fruit of knowledge. A question has been asked us, will the brinker landlords - viz Lord Dynevor, B. Hall Esq, M.P., J. Bassett, Esq., Mrs Morgan, the Hon R. H. Clive, and the Marquis of Bute, permit the Bards to protect and preserve their temple! Our answer has been, and is, WE HAVE NO DOUBT they will not only charter our prescriptive right to protect the Druid's temple, but express their sense of approbation by directing their names to be added to the list of subscribers for its preservation:

> "One common cause makes millions of one breast,
> Slaves of the East, or Helots of the West;
> On Andes' or on Athos' peaks unfurll'd,
> The self-same standard streams o'er either world."

"As some may question the applicability of the word Temple, at the present day, to designate an immense rude and poisted fragment of the Rock, on an elevated plain, with no other covering than that of the sky, I beg leave most humbly to submit, that it is infinitely more deserving of that term, than the Temple of Jupiter Ammon, in Thebes. As none will dispute, I think Thomson's description of this Temple, not made with hands, I shall give it here, to illustrate this opinion - he sings:

> "Nature attend! Join every living soul,
> Beneath the spacious Temple of the sky
> In adoration join; and ardent raise
> One general song!"

"In this, and in similar temples, the music, the language and institutions of the Britons, made their first impressions on the infant and savage brain. In this, and in similar temples, civilisation was born, nursed and educated under the tuition of men of genius. In this, and similar temples, the uncivilised Britons first acknowledged the dominion of the superior intelligence.

"In this temple, the bards received their degrees of proficiency in the arts and sciences from age to age, from time immemorial to the present day. In this, and in similar temples, opinion, the Queen of the universe, was created to govern the rulers of the earth.

"As Y Maen Chwyf then is *the* temple where civilisation was born, let the modern Britons of all grades of opinion second the motion of the Cymreigyddion Society of Newbridge, with the means to protect and preserve to the latest posterity, this sublime temple of antiquity, where, perhaps, the remains of the Genius of Serch Hudol and Gadlys lie buried unknown.

"Let the respect and reverence we owe to the unknown benefactors of mankind inspire us with gratitude to preserve and protect Y Maen Chwyf, as a monument of their superior intelligence.

"Let Y Maen Chwyf be the banner of civilisation, around which millions, yet unborn, shall assemble to learn the music, the language, and institutions of the Britons. Here stands the Temple, wide as the horizon is, high as heaven is, infinite as time is, where all shades of opinion shall never blush to assembly "in the face of day, and in the eye of light!"

"And see!
Tis come, the glorious morn! The second birth
Of heaven on earth! Awakening nature hears
The new creating word, and starts to life,
In every heightened form, from pain and death
For ever free!"

A century before the first Museum of Welsh Life would open in St Fagans, near Cardiff, Price had already thought of it. Subscriptions were received by Phillip Thomas, manager of The Ynysangharad Works, who was elected treasurer with a special account opened by the West of England and South Wales District Bank and by the Merthyr Bank. Dr Price was the secretary. The list of patrons was led by Francis Crawshay who donated £1. 1s and Price with £10.10s. Also on the list was his own brother and sister, Charles and Anne, then residing in the address of Primrose Bank, Newbridge.

The total subscriptions of 157 were promised at £131 17s 11d. It was quite a large sum of money at the time and hardly an amount to be scoffed at. Sadly, the scheme foundered for lack of support among other industrialists in the area and the money was never collected.

The entire project was a failure, possibly due to the fact that Price was already showing some signs of sympathy to the growing cause of Chartism, making him increasingly unpopular with the wealthier members of the community whose donations he needed.

Dr Price wrote an angry letter to the *Cardiff and Merthyr Guardian* on September 21, 1839, "I imagined like a child there would be no difficulty in inspiring the whole length and breadth of Britain a 1,000 ladies and gentlemen to subscribe a sovereign each.

But to my great astonishment, I found they were biased to think or suspect I was inspired by some sinister motives. I see a vote in the House of Commons in granting £70,000 for repairing the Queen's stables for a few horses and but £30,000 of people's own money to educate a whole nation of 26 million laughing me in the face."

In 1853, he held a fund-raising tea party at the Rocking Stone in an effort to help pay for a new bridge to cross the river Taff, near Edward's famous old bridge. Earlier that year, applications were made to solicitor Edward Colnett Spickett for the new bridge to be built by Glamorgan Quarter Sessions. The old bridge could not cope with the streams of carts and carriages travelling to the Glamorganshire Canal. Postmaster Charles Bassett (who was responsible for changing the name of Newbridge to Pontypridd in 1856), formed a committee to raise a public subscription, and meetings were held at the Tredegar Arms. To aid publicity, a hot-air balloon was launched from a field adjacent to the gasworks across the river

A local reputation as a brilliant physician and surgeon ensued, despite Dr. Price's heretical beliefs and eschewal of convention, be it medical, social, or religious. Whether his behaviour was merely quirky, or a manifestation of mental illness, remains the subject of speculation. He was clearly a maverick and a rebel, and his bizarre behaviour led him into frequent conflict with the law and the Church.

While working at Brown Lenox, he devised an embryonic national health service – 125 years before today's National Health was launched – with a system of payment whereby workers paid him when they were well and he treated them for free when they were ill. Equally, he felt that fellow physicians should only be paid when someone is healed, otherwise they could allow a patient to remain sick for a long time to ensure they received more money out of them for treatment! Contemptuous of the rest of his profession, whom he saw as poison peddlers preying on the sick, Price dispensed herbal remedies to treat conditions rather than relieve symptoms, throwing in Druidic incantations for good measure. His reputation as a healer, however, went before him and people continually turned to him as a leading physician, despite his Druidic beliefs. He strongly condemned the practice of inoculation and experiments on animals, instead advocating vegetarianism, good food, clean living, fresh air, exercise and natural medicine.

He absolutely refused to treat smokers. In fact, on one journey by train from Merthyr to Pontypridd it was reported that Price asked a fellow passenger not to smoke. When he refused, Price grabbed his clay pipe and threw it through the open window. Then he threatened to throw the smoker out as well if he continued to protest. As a strict vegetarian, he believed "that the eating of animal flesh has a tendency to revive in men the worst passions of the brute. I contend that human beings ought not to eat animal food, and the Cymmerian teachers forbade it. The man who eats animal food descends to the level of the brute, and will in time aquire the habits and passions of a beast."

He regarded vaccination as "a method established by law for the express purpose of slaughtering infants." It was hardly a surprising outburst, remembering the death of his brother at such a young age from a vaccination.

"We are suffering under the curse of the past mistakes of our profession. We have been educating the public into the false belief that poisonous drugs can give health. This belief has become such a deep-rooted superstition, that those of us who know better and who would like to adopt more rational methods, can only do so at the risk of losing our practice and reputation. The average doctor is at his best but a devoted bigot to this damnable teaching which we call the medical art, and which alone in this age of science, has made no perceptible progress since the days of its earliest teachers. Some call it recognised science. I call it ignorance!"

He never lost his contempt for medicines and pills or expressing radical views on nudity, free love and unusual style of dress, coupled by a desire to wash every coin in his possession and his refusal to wear socks on hygienic grounds. It was certainly a trait adopted by his son a century later. He said "Stockings prevent the proper exhalation of the feet, which, in consequence, are kept damp; and the person who wears them is more liable to catch cold. My feet are always dry and warm." A keen walker, he was known to visit his patients at night, riding or walking ten or fifteen miles in the early hours, his theory being that people were at their worst at night and needed more attention than during the day. He never wore a watch, which he said was not needed in his profession as the time to see patients was "when they send for you."

It was at Brown Lenox that he was said to have performed a bone-graft operation on an injured worker from the leg of a calf. He was also a major influence in setting up the first co-operative in Wales, the 'Pontypridd Provision Company', to break the stranglehold that the shopkeepers had on the workers. Sadly, it failed just eighteen months later after he offered too much credit following one of the many strikes in the area. Another of his dreams had failed, but the need for social reform was more evident than ever and Price, ever the crusader, began to show clear signs of political activism.

Chapter Four
THE CHARTIST

CHARTISM pierced the very heart of parliamentary reform. It was established and controlled by working men to achieve parliamentary democracy as a step towards social and economic change. It symbolised an unrest amongst the industrial areas of the working classes, and its demands fired the imagination of the more militant and rebellious temperament of its campaigners. The Six Points of the Charter embodied many of the principles which Dr Price had been advocating for years, such as universal male suffrage, annual parliaments, secret ballot, equal electoral districts, salaries for MPs and the abolition of property qualifications for MPs. Terrible social conditions led to the revolt. Since the 1790s, the industrial valleys had been a culture of alienation, sedition and violent protests, and the workers had plenty to protest about. Throughout Britain, men, women and children worked 14 hours a day for little reward. For a time, workers looked to the Radicals in Parliament, but the much talked-about Reform Act of 1832 still only gave votes to the rich. It was a huge disappointment. In June 1836, the London Working Men's Association was formed and in 1838, the members launched a People's Charter and National Petition, which called for radical changes to the way in which Britain was governed. From then on, supporters of the movement were known as Chartists. In 1838, the call for the People's Charter was made, compiling all six points into an official document, along with a large petition. Parliament refused it.

Leading chartist John Frost, a magistrate from Newport, said that the working man should "look to no one but himself, for if he depends on those who are in superior situations, he will always be disappointed." The People's Charter was foremost in his mind and the campaigning began. Chartism is often dismissed as only being about reform of the polling system, but it was much, much more. Workers thought that when the charter was law, their lives would be transformed for the better

They believed that "children would no longer labour . . . men and women would only work for six hours a day . . . the distinctions between rich and poor would be swept away."

After Parliament rejected the petition, leaders like Frost, then on trial for treason, and Henry Vincent, called for physical force to obtain it. South Wales was to be the storm centre. Months of painstaking work went into preparing for the planned insurrection and Frost and Vincent travelled all over England and Wales calling on workers to 'look to yourselves to get the Charter'.

After being replaced as mayor of Newport, Frost concentrated his efforts in campaigning. At the National Chartist Convention, he emerged as one of the leaders of the Physical Force Chartist. Lord John Russell, the Home Secretary, was appalled when he discovered that a magistrate was advocating the use of violence. In March 1839, the Home Secretary decided to have Frost removed as a Newport magistrate.

The Chartist riot in Newport

Price does not seem to have been involved in the earlier Merthyr Rising of 1831, but he did support Josiah John Guest, the ironmaster of Dowlais, during the Merthyr elections of 1834 when Guest, the nominee for the Radicals, fought off a challenge from the town's Tories. This activity must have brought Price into contact with the future leaders of Merthyr Chartism and when in 1839 the Chartist's campaign grew into a mass movement in South Wales, Price soon became enthusiastically involved. When it came to finding a natural born leader who enjoyed the respect of the people in Pontypridd and valleys, the Chartists looked no further than Dr Price himself.

Events earlier in the year had started peacefully enough. On April 22, 1839, accompanied by two hundred little boys and girls, Henry Vincent (who was later imprisoned) and Dr Price proceeded to Blackwood and on arriving at the Coach and Horses public house, they began their business with a local committee. Price was called to the chair and opened the meeting in a Welsh speech full of eloquence and argument, concluding, amidst loud cheers from the crowd of 3,000 people, with a quotation from the "Rights of Man".

Dr Price was appointed leader of Pontypridd and lower Rhondda branch of the country-wide movement, holding meetings at the Rocking Stone, where he often gave stirring speeches, which lasted two hours on the night he was elected leader.

His commitment to the Welsh language, which he spoke eloquently, was steadfast. Every Sunday morning in the "Commonwealth Society Hall of the Industrious People of Great Britain", an unlicensed beer house on the Ynysybwl Road to Llanwonno, he organised Welsh classes, only to see them broken up by the police, who suspected them of being a cover for lessons in the handling of muskets and military training.

On May 6, 1839, Captain Howells of Cardiff, adjutant of the Royal Glamorgan Militia, wrote to the Marquis of Bute (1793-1848), the Lord Lieutenant of Glamorgan, and warned "that the person who was agitating about Nantgarw was a surgeon attending Mr Crawshay's works at Newbridge (Pontypridd), and had always been considered a strange, flighty character." The Marquis was further informed by T. W. Booker of Velindre that Mr Stacey had told him "that the leaders of the Chartists in this neighbourhood, viz, a surgeon of the name of Price, who resides near Newbridge, and a shopkeeper called Davies of Dinas, with two dissenting preachers, have been extremely motive among the colliers of the parish of Llanvabon, and likewise at Blackwood during the past week."

On July 12, 1839, the petition for the Charter with a quarter-million signatures was rejected by the ruling class in Parliament by 235 votes to 46. It was obvious their attempts had failed. Frost, Taylor of Birmingham, Bussey of Yorkshire, and other leaders, met in secret and decided the only alternative to reach their goal was by physical force.

On August 12, Dr Price was in the chair at a large Chartist meeting of 2,500 people in Duke's Town, Tredegar. During an open-air meeting in Cefn Cribwr, a member of the local gentry, mounted on his horse, demanded the speeches were given in the Queen's English, not in Welsh. As he attacked the chairman of the meeting, it was Dr Price who rushed to defend him. On August 18, 1839, from the Court House in Merthyr, Mr William Thomas wrote to the Marquis of Bute that Price was "a fit subject, in the opinion of most, for a lunatic asylum." According to one source, Price spent time in September on a political tour of Staffordshire and the North of England.

At the same time, the Cardiff Reform Association had asked Dr Price to help them in registering for voters. His reply in a letter speaks for itself: "The battle of the country for equal laws and fair play is to be fought in the brains of the working classes and not in the registration counts as the Whigs and the Tories would have us believe. I have nothing to do with Whigs or Tories and liken them to players at a card game. Just as card players throw away a pack of cards when it becomes old and dirty, so the Whigs and the Tories condemn people to the workhouse when they can no longer work or fight for their masters. Both parties permit living off the industries of the people and inciting nations to war against each other."

Dr John Taylor, the Scottish Chartist leader, had heard Price had been chosen to lead an armed insurrection in Wales. Price had seven pieces of cannon in his possession and Taylor also organised a supply of small arms for trained hands - with the business help of Richard Cule, a shopkeeper in Treforest. On September 6, 1839, the magistrates of Lower Miskin reported the quantity of firearms, including several packages of double-barrelled pistols worth 30 shillings each, powder flasks and bullet moulds.

Again, Captain, Howells informed the Marquis that Price and Davies were the two most dangerous people living in the area and a close eye needed to be kept on both of them. By the end of October 1839, Frost, William Jones, a journeyman watchmaker and innkeeper Zephaniah Williams organised a march in Newport. It is generally acknowledged that Frost and other Chartist leaders did not agree on the course of action adopted and quite possibly Price realised that the utter chaos that ensued could result in casualties. It seems as if Frost realised the English Chartists were not as prepared to take matters in their own hands as the Welsh.

On the one hand he wanted to lead the Welsh Chartists, on the other he needed to hold them back. Six weeks beforehand, Frost called a meeting at Twyn y Star, Blaenau Gwent, which Price attended. Frost asked them to rise together at his bidding. David Davies of Abersychan, a Waterloo veteran, who held a lodge of 1,600 which included 1,200 soldiers, said they would rise if they had specific instructions and knew of a list of men they were to kill (or "remove"). Frost promised to acquire such a list before the rising. It never came.

Strangely enough, despite his position in the Chartist movement in Wales, Price did not attend the march, probably because of a personal disagreement with Frost over his methods of protest. In truth, it appeared that Price was suspicious of him all along. Years later, he condemned Frost for keeping his men out in the rain on the day of the march, calling him a traitor since he believed Frost was allowing the army time to fill the Westgate pub – the centre of the upheaval - before their arrival. This is probably very unfair. Price was elderly and more prone to delusions when he made some of his most outlandish claims. Quite simply, there was no master plan and Price knew best not to get involved.

On October 26, he was requested to meet Frost at his apartment. It was obvious that Price distrusted him and thought a listener was also in the room. This may have been part of Price's paranoia, of course. Price would only whisper, and still Frost would not reveal the full plan for the march. Frost would not consider slaughtering the army that awaited their men, unlike Price who was prepared to kill "a hundred thousand if necessary." Price cursed Frost, adding, "You shall not put a sword in my hand and a rope around my neck at the same time. If I take a sword in my hand, I will use it, and no one shall take it from me but at the cost of my life."

Later, it was claimed that soldiers had been informed beforehand to "shoot the man with the long hair". Price, normally the crusader, broke himself off totally with the Chartists before the riot and had no intention to take any further part in the proceedings. In later interviews with Ap Ifandryn, he said: "If the chartists had only been properly commanded, they could have carried everything before them."

On the wet and windy night of November 3, 1839, the capitalist class in South Wales was in a blind panic. Mine owners hid themselves down their own pits. "Men

The Newport Rising of 1839

of property took to their heels" and fled to the fields with their families. One minister of religion spent the night in a pond. They were told, "The Chartists are coming".

Several thousand workers, armed with muskets, pikes and clubs, were marching on Newport. They planned to free the political prisoners held in the Westgate Hotel and proclaim a Silurian Republic. Victory at Newport would be the signal for a nationwide uprising.

The result was a disaster in both political and military terms. A brief, violent, and bloody battle ensued. Shots were fired by both sides, although most contemporaries agree that the soldiers holding the building had vastly superior firepower. The Chartists did manage to enter the building temporarily, but were forced to retreat in disarray: twenty were killed, another fifty wounded.

After 25 minutes, the Chartists were driven off by a 4,000-strong army of redcoats in waiting, who fired into the crowd. In the aftermath, some 200 people were arrested for taking part in the rising. John Frost, Zephaniah Williams and William Jones were sentenced to be hanged, drawn and quartered, though because of public pressure they were transported for life to Tasmania. After being granted a full pardon in 1856, Frost returned to England and, until his death at Stapleton, near Bristol, on July 27, 1877, devoted his last two decades to writing and lecturing, mainly on the horrors of deportation.

Concern was growing about the other leaders who could exert such power over the men. It was obvious that Price had to escape and – according to a later interview – a £100 reward for him, dead or alive, was announced. This has never been substantiated, however. According to further correspondence between Captain Howells and the Marquis of Bute, Price disappeared by October 25. Price later said, "The authorities were afraid of another Chartist rising and so they deemed it wise to secure me and others if they could. They knew very well that the men of Merthyr and Aberdare would do anything at my bidding."

The police were certainly aware of his influence in the valleys and ensured the Welsh ports were closed in an effort to catch the doctor. On November 28, W. Coffin of Llandaff also wrote to the Marquis, claiming, "I am satisfied that the whole of the bad spirit in this district is to be attributed to Price and W. David. He has been sowing poison in the minds of all around him. I understand a warrant is out against Price by the Monmouthshire justices."

William David of Dinas, whose father had founded a Baptist chapel there, was believed to have fled to America. Price told an exciting tale of his movement after a warrant had been issued for his arrest. Obviously, before he began growing a lengthy beard, the clean-shaven doctor, disguised as a woman, managed to escape aboard a Liverpool-bound vessel at Cardiff.

Police Inspector Stockdale was on special duty at the docks and carried a warrant for his arrest. According to Price, the inspector assisted a lady on the deck, who was none other than Price himself. He went below, then reappeared as a man, but still disguised. When the ship stopped at Milford Haven he had a look around the town and enjoyed a drink in the Nelson Hotel. It was there that a stranger made conversation with him and Price began to suspect something was afoot. It was none other than the master of the port, sent to talk to him by the captain of the ship, who was suspicious of Price.

It would appear that the stranger offered to show Dr Price around the town while hoping the warrant would arrive in time. But the warrant was too long in coming and the ship had to sail out or miss the tide. When well out to sea, a furious Price sent for Captain Edwards, knowing he'd revealed his identity to the authorities and warned him "If ever I meet you on shore, I shall whip the life out of you."

On reaching Liverpool, he travelled to London by rail. It is pure speculation that Dr Price did not escape to France at all, but was merely hidden away by Francis Crawshay in a secret chamber discovered in 1940 under the floor of what used to be Forest House. In truth, Price was destined for France and, a few days after reaching London, he continued his escape in disguise, by steamer, to Le Havre and finally arrived in Paris. Once on safe shores, he penned a little note to Constable Stockdale, who unwittingly helped the disguised doctor on board the ship, to wish him well and thank him for his assistance!

At Paris, he was said to have met a college friend, John Masklyn, a doctor who had married a French woman and offered Price a room in their apartment.

During his lengthy stay, Dr Price claimed to have become a close friend to Captain Phelps, the brother-in-law of King Louis Philippe. Phelps was said to have married the king's sister, and originally came from Cottrell, near Cowbridge. He once owned a £20,000 estate in North Wales. Ironically, a Phelps surname does appear in the family history of King Philip IV of France. Unfortunately, that monarch reigned five centuries earlier!

Taking Price under his wing, Phelps introduced the Welsh doctor to a host of his closest friends, who included the exiled philosopher, Heinrich Heine, the German writer and one of the strangest characters in literary history. Born in Dusseldorf, of Jewish origin, his poems inspired such composers as Mendelssohn, Schubert, and Schumann. Through him, Price allegedly met the 79-year-old Dr Christian Samuel Frederich Hahnemann, regarded as the ultimate father of homeopathy. He talked about the Vital Force or the Vital Energy, ridiculed at that time but now accepted. His scientific mind was neither satisfied nor convinced of the effectiveness of the existing medical practices, which he felt did more harm than good to the patients. Dr Price was in awe of him, learning of the benefits of natural herbs and plants for cure and believing the body had the capacity for self-healing.

More than half a century later, Price was asked by Ap Idanfryn about his time in Paris and questioned whether he ever actually met King Louis Philippe. "Oh yes, I used to see him almost every day at the palace," he quipped. "I often had a friendly chat with him. It was at His Majesty's particular request that I visited him and I remember that he used to laugh heartily when I told him how I had escaped the English police."

During Price's exile, he took interest in Captain Phelps's 16-year-old daughter, Yvonne, a beautiful and accomplished girl. The captain assumed they would marry and so Price was allowed access to society of a high standing. But the connection with Phelps was ended when Price enjoyed taking the girl to the country, undressing her and caressing her nude body. Understandably, Price was banished from the Phelps household.

The time had come, once more, to consider returning to Wales, but not before receiving a vision which would ultimately change his life.

A touch of Ancient Wales.

Chapter Five
THE ARCHDRUID

DURING the stay in France, Dr Price's mind undeniably began showing signs of a severe mental disorder, making his fantasies all the more extreme. Given he was in his late thirties, it was almost as if family history was repeating itself, since his father showed similar signs at the same age. In later life, his preposterous claim that all Greek books were the work of the early Welsh bards and Homer had been born at Caerphilly – and built the town's castle – naturally confirmed this, let alone the bizarre, rambling documents in an unfathomable form of Welsh language.

But even in these earlier years of his life, there is an eccentricity about him that can only be described as the early onset of a mental problem. He relied on the authority of the Myvirian Archaeology of Wales and began to immerse himself in the Cult of Druidism. Druidry in its early form was dedicated to the love of the land, the earth and nature. As peacemakers, they planted peace groves, held ceremonies praising beauty, justice and truth. Also their love of animals, the body, sun, moon, stars and sky shows clearly Dr Price's total dedication to the rich Druidic heritage. Even the Druid's love of stones by building stone circles and collecting stones and crystals can rather ironically remind us of the late Reverend Price's eccentricities. Did he really hold Druidic beliefs like his son? It would explain the reason behind casting aside his position in the Anglican church. Or was his love of stones merely symbolic of a poor mental state? One which could have easily crept into the mind of a young William?

The Druids and Druidesses formed the professional class in Celtic society. They performed the functions of modern-day priests, teachers, ambassadors, astronomers, genealogists, philosophers, musicians, theologians, scientists, poets and judges. They underwent lengthy training, some sources say twenty years.

The Christian Church absorbed much of Celtic religion: many Pagan Gods and Goddesses became Christian saints; sacred springs and wells were preserved and associated with saints; many Pagan temple sites became the location of cathedrals. By the 7th century, Druidism itself was destroyed or continued deeply underground throughout most of the formerly Celtic lands.

It was amidst this wealth of Druidic history in which Price immersed himself that he visited the Louvre Gallery in Paris, where he saw a Greek stone bearing a portrait of the primitive bard addressing the moon. According to Druidic traditions, they acted as priests to the immigrant Celts and the bard was an order of Druid whose office was to supervise, regulate and to lead. According to Dr Price's later writings, he believed the precious stone was in existence for 2,000 years but claimed that he, and only he, could decipher the inscription in hieroglyphics.

The stone, which he called Gwylllis yn Nayd (The Will of My Father), depicted a Druid addressing the moon while holding Coelbren y Beirdd in one hand (the Bardic Alphabet) and in the other a mundane egg, the image of immortality. Price was obsessed with the object and from it prophesied that one day a child would be born, called Mab Duw (Son of God) and he would rule the new earth under Druidic law.

It was an incredible prophecy according to Price, illustrating that once again a new Christ would reign over the earth and the ancient Druidic system be restored. Without question, Price felt that it would be his first-born son who would be crowned a Druidic Messiah and restore the system to its ancient glory. Price named himself the ArchDruid of Wales, or the Son of the Primitive Bard, and from him would come the next ruler of the earth.

Dr Price wrote, "The Primitive Bard, you know, represents himself as the source of the ocean. Perhaps, you have noticed that one of the emblems of Freemasonry is a board with water flowing out of its centre - that, really, represents the Primitive Bard. It is said that it was Newton who discovered that the moon influenced the movement of the sea, but that was well known to the Druids thousands of years before he was born."

Price wrote of the stone some forty years later: "I should tell you that during my stay in Paris in 1839 I visited the Louvre, and there came across a precious stone, on which was inscribed the portrait of the primitive bard in the act of addressing the moon. In one hand he holds Coelbren y Beirdd while in the other he has a mundane egg.

"Across the body I found inscribed several Greek characters and hieroglyphics and although the stone has been in existence for 2,000 years, I am the only person who has been able to decipher the inscription, and I spent twenty years of my life doing so.

"The characters represent the Song of the Primitive Bard, the theme of which is Iesu Grist, and he says that his son shall walk on earth again as before. Now, although I have given a challenge and publicly offered £50 to anyone who would be able to decipher the song, no one except myself has been able to do so.

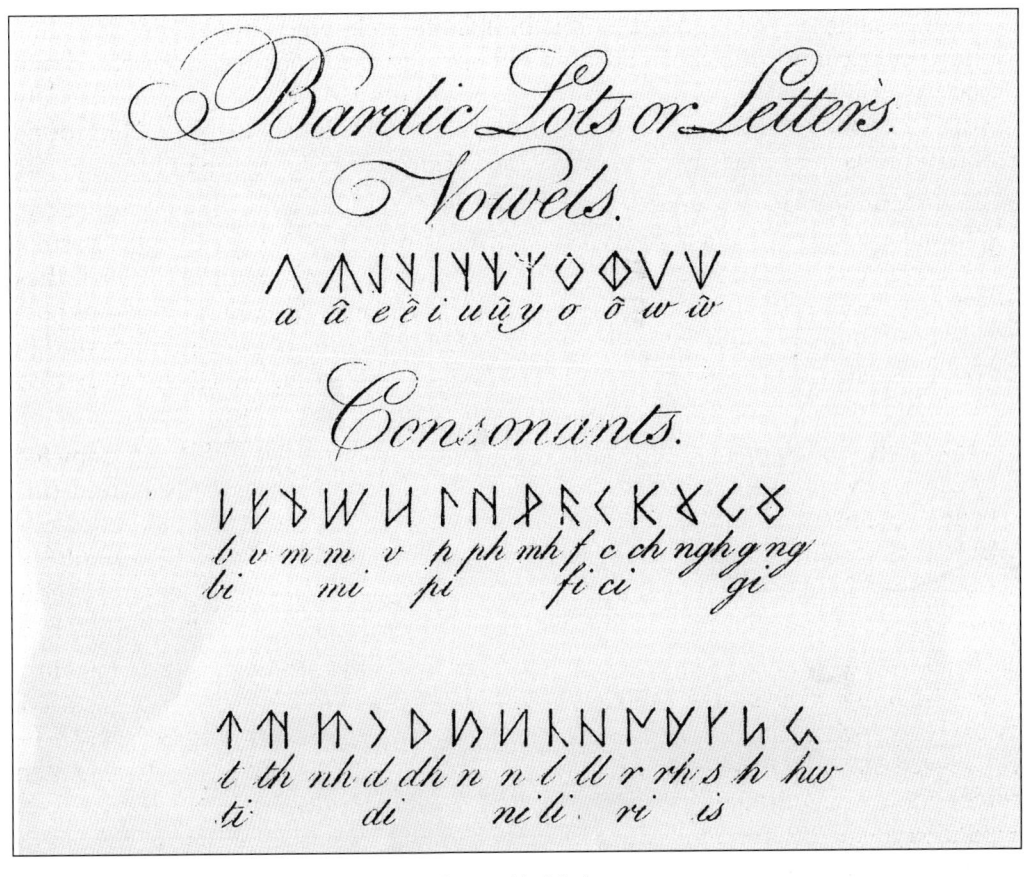

The Druid alphabet

I am the son of the Primitive Bard, and it is this son of mine, Iesu Grist, that the bards sings about. I therefore call it Gwyllllis yn Nayd."

This is the translation that Price offered of the tablet on the right hand side of the bard:

"Has thou seen the strong Lord
The black rod of song of the Lords,
That sows hell
With my old ocean for the sun to generate me?
He will liberate my country
The lord in judgement!
Enslaved in my temple that gathers whomsoever you are to serve him who is
Yes, who is! "A" that will go before "A" I sowed my seed in
The limit of the blockhead God that has no seed in him!
"A" will go before I shall cease to shed the blood of armies.
"A" will go before the inglorious foam shall come on my lips
"A" will go before the equivalent power shall come on the wooden wands
Of the poet my soul "A" will be my equivalent seed
The administrator of my will in the letters of books

GWYLLLLIS YN NAYD.

"Yn Tayd wut Ti yn y Nevvoydd! Sancttudd vyddddo dy Ennw Di dyet dy Dyrrnnas! Byddddet dy Wyllllis Di arr ydd Ddauarr meggis ym ma I yn y Nevvoydd! Dyrro inni eddddu yn Barra Bynnyddddiol A madddda yn Dyled Diou vel ym madddduwnni yu Dyledwurr! Na arrwinni u Brorvidigayth yuththurr ynggwarred Ni rayg yd Drwgg! Cannis dy yudddot Ti uw yd Dyrrnnas yg gallllu a yryggogonniant yn oys oyssoydd A ym Menn! A ym Menn! A ym Menn!"

Arryggraphphwyd I gann Dr. William Price o yb Bont y Priyth Ymmorryggannwg A ych choyvrrestrwyd I yn Neuadd yll Lleennoggion yn yll Llynndann Dudd Albann Arrththann 1871.

The cover of Gwyllllis Yn Nayd, published by Dr Price in 1871

In the custody of my tongue after I shall see myself liberated
In the might of those who will hunt out my bard's books
Who will buy the country of heaven to sow my supreme seed
They will buy the country of heaven who will sow my supreme seed.
And a common primitive bard

And here is the translation of the tablet on the left of the bard:-

I am a divine
And a common primitive bard
Who knows every songster
In the cave of seasons
I will liberate the place where I am confined
In the belly of the stone tower
I will tell your king
And the common people
That wonderful animal will come
From the shores of the Lord of War
To punish the lies of the bloodhounds of mankind.
I will go into his hair, his teeth and his eyes of gold in peace.
And I will visit with vengeance their lives on the bloodhounds of mankind."

Gwyllllis yn Nayd, the fruit of an overactive, or even slightly insane, imagination was published by Dr Price in London on "Dudd Alben Arrththann 1871". Although the publication was released thirty years after his trip to Paris, showing signs of the decline of his mental state at times, there is no doubt that he showed such signs as far back as 1840, although obviously not as severely. Gwyllllis yn Nayd was his philosophy of Druidism, the code which he lived by. The title is a corruption of Ewyllys Fy Nhad (The Will of My Father) and on the cover is a corrupted version of the Lord's Prayer in the same curious semi-phonetic Welsh, with quadrupled consonants.

He believed it was the original Welsh language spoken 2,600 years before. Sometimes poetic, very disjointed and fragmentary, he claimed it should not be translated – but when it is, it remains equally as elusive. Beneath is embossed a red goat, surrounded by a green serpent with its tail in its mouth and itself encircled with the letters IUYUAIUYUEUOYUS. This crest he used on his private notepaper, and the goat was also represented on his brass buttons. He had it struck in bronze to commemorate the cremation of Iesu Grist.

This was undoubtedly his greatest fantasy. The text is rambling and confused, but the direction of his concern is clear. He emphasises he is addressing the Welsh people in correct Welsh in order to reveal the "Song of the Wan of the Lettered Lore of the Welsh" which he has discovered after 2,000 years. The will of his father, he says, "has been kept secret during the time of the foreign kings for their own advantage to mis-rule the nations of the earth. Remember that the living god himself is born a Welshman in his natural memory."

Anwyl Gymmru a Chymmressi!

Vi uw yb Barrydd Llyththyrrennog
Ang gnoyul Brenn yn ym Llaww!
Yd dorra Gayn yv Vronnvraith
A yrr Ettudd arr y Wawrr!
E A S T S O W Th
W E S T N O R Th!
E A A A u Maththu I
Yll Lluad oyurr yn Varra Chaws!

    W I yn ych cyvvarchchi yn Llyththyrrennog ynggymmrayg " yd Dalith Vrenninol " yn ym moydd yc clwwas I ym Mamm a yn Nayd yn wlua Cymmrayg o ym mayb Banndoyd u ysbbyssu ubboyb Clust Cymmro a Chymmrays Taw dymma ym moydd yll Llyththyrrennwys Privv Varrydd Duscc Cymmru " Gayn Coyul Brenn Duscc Lyththyrrennog yc Cymmru ys wedu Dwu Viyl a wech cant o vlynnydddda u yn ol y welwchchi arr ynggwiscc I wedu choppio Lyththyrrun wth Llyththyrrun A Lleww Llouyggarr arr ym ol o yrr Ail Rann o yl " L'Antiquité Expliquée arryggraphphwyd yn Parris yn 1722 gann Dom Bernard DeMontfaucon."

    W I wedu Llanno yt Tri Gwall y wela I arr wnnwg yp Privv Varrydd Duscc o yt Tri Llyththyrrun " E V V " a ych chuvlyththyrrennu poyb Arrwuddddion Llevverrudd W I yn u welad yn y Wi a ych chuvlyththyrrennu poyb Llyththyrrun y welwch chiththa o yg Gayn ynggywwirr yn yll Llyththyrrenna su yn cayl u dysccu yn yrr Ysccol Lion Cymmrayg yn Bressennol arr yd Daul Cannlynnol u ych cyvvarryddwuddddochchi dduall a darrllin a channu " Cayn Coyul Brenn Privv Varrydd Duscc Cymmru yn Llyththyrrennog yn ol yc Cyvvarryddwuddddion a ych chuvlyththyrrenna yg Gayn yn y Wi y wela I arr " yg Groyn yd Duun yg Gerrws u unan" yg Glwssoch chiththa lawwar o ys Soyn amm Danno!!!

    I E! Anwyl Gymmru a Chymmressi! " Croyn yd Duun yg Gerrws u unan!!!" Gwuddddochchi pwun nuw E? Oys Neyb o ychchi yn attebb? Nayg oys Neyb! Vi wetta wththochchi ynnta!" Croyn yn Nayd I a ych Tayd chiththa yc Cymmru Anwyl uw " Croyn yd Duun yg Gerrws u unan" yn Draggwuddddol ynggophphadwrriaith yc Cymmru y welwchchi arr ynggroyn I A ych choppi o Wyllllis yn Tayd Ni arrnno Aws E oyu Mennudd u unan yn Llyththyrrennog o yrr Oyul trw yll Lluad arr ym Moryr ac arr ydd Ddauarr oyu Laww Dde mwnn Wi'oyurr yn Dywyssog Traggwuddddol arr yu Vyibbonn H E Th " yn Ennw yd Duw Ayphphoyb Daioni " ynggymmrayg " yd Dalith Vrenninol"—Cymmrayg Gwent A Moryrgannwg yn yv Vlwuddddun 1871 yn ol Creyd—Ddaytguddddiad u Wyllllis oyu Wi oyurr Il Lien E su wedu cayl u chattw yn ddirrgel ynggysttud Brenninoydd Dieiththriaid arr yu Llees u unain u gammllywodrayththu Cynnedloydd ydd Ddauarr oyu Annvoydd wth Anggen u Ela Ettivvedd Gwyllllis yn Tayd Ni yn Ennw uv Vayb E yb Bia yc Cledddddu ollalluog ac oll Gyvvoyththog ydd Ddycewd arr yu Vyibbonn H E Th Rryvval Draggwuddddol ynggalonna Cynnedloydd Lledieith nuys dychchwelannw yc Cledddddu uddu Laww E yb Bia Lywodrayththu yn eddychlonn arr Orrsedd yrr Oyul arr ydd Ddauarr yn Draggwuddddol Ovvoydd Saith Synnwrr Anianol yc Cymmru arr ddudd yu Gened Digayth o Wi oyurr Il Lien E!!!

    Coyvviwchchi voyd yd Duw Buw u unan yn Genni yng Gymmro yn u Goyv Anianol yn Blant yr oll Gynnedloydd arr ddudd yu Gened Digayth o yg Groyth ayu Saith Synnwrr Anianol gannththo Ve yn Draggwuddddol.

                    Ve Goyvvia!
                      Ve Gluww!
                      Ve Levv!
                      Ve Vlassa!
                      Ve Dymmyla
                      Ve weyl!
                      Ve yth Annal yd Duw Buw u unan oyu Phroynna Ve o yg Groyth yn Draggwuddddol Ebb Dduscc yd Duw Dayd Bettudd—ma Ennw arrall arr yd Duw Dayd Bettudd

The opening page of Gwyllllis Yn Nayd, published in almost unfathomable Welsh in 1871. This was his philosophy of Druidism.

The second half of the document contains Price's greatest fantasy – an eisteddfod of a million Welsh men and women, on the slopes of Snowdon, with himself at the centre repeating in the form of a catechism questions intended to show the Welsh origin of all things. He sums up his claim that "I have proof positive I am the son of the Welsh Primitive Bard and I am equally certain that this second child of mine, whom I have called Iesu Grist, will reign on earth, and that in him the ancient Druidical system will be restored."

Price was unquestionably not of balanced mind. Within its pages, there are also drawings of the original stone he claims to have seen at the Louvre so many years earlier. Overall, its contents are written in the most bizarre, elusive form of Welsh, with one translated section reading:

> "Dear Welshmen and Welshwomen.
> I am the lettered bard
> With my wand in my hand
> Which breaks the song of the thrush
> And the lark on the dawn
> East South
> West North
> The cold moon bread and cheese."

Quite obviously, it makes little sense to us, but for Dr Price it was his divine scripture. In later years, Ap Idanfryn was shown a verse printed on a card bearing a portrait of Iesu Grist Price, the son Price cremated in 1884. This was "the pedigree of Jesus Christ", but Dr Price would not explain what it meant, for if he did, "There would be a great commotion among the learned men in all countries. That verse contains a reference to the ages, the mouth and other organs of man, but you must not tell this to the physiologists."

As Dr John Cule explained in his 1960 thesis of Price, "Although written in a type of Welsh that even the Welsh speakers themselves could not understand, Price further warns those who read it that they are forbidden to translate it. When it is translated, the content is just as elusive!

"Like the ramblings of a disintegrating schizophrenic, you can recognise the education and cultural background of Price, even if it has become fragmented and inconsequential. However, the Will of My Father is a unique document, and Price used it subsequently as a substantiation for his delusions because he felt the need to provide some explanation for his extraordinary claims of inheritance. The fact he felt the necessity to produce this proof at all is evidence of his uncertainty about his fantasy."

Few would argue Dr Price's flamboyance or for that matter his total arrogance, too. It was a facet of his character epitomised by his style of costume with bright reds and green, creating a startling image as a priest of his sun god. Wearing the foxskin on his head, the brush stitched to the upper part of the pelt, similar to the one he claimed was worn by the primitive bard depicted on the ancient stone, the tails and legs were draped about his shoulders, symbolising his emblem as a healer.

Dymma Rann o yrr yp Plann ym ma yn Nayd yn ug Gannu u yth thu "A" "yth Annal El yth Llevvei ov."

Part of the inscription found on the Greek stone at the Louvre, Paris, and allegedly "translated" by Dr Price.

Two of the emblems from Gwyllllis Yn Nayd

Although a short man, he made up for his size with his colourful head dress. He said to Ap Idanfryn: "The fox is represented as one of the first beings in the heiroglyphics of Egypt. The primitive bard and the Druids always wore foxskin head coverings."

The colours of his outfit were also based on Druidic lore and undoubtedly he followed some of the examples of Iolo Morganwg. He claimed the Ovate wore green, typifying verdant spring and Price had trousers made of the same colour. The bard wore sky blue, typifying the summer and the Druid wore white, the colour of his tunic, typifying old age and sanctity.

He also allowed his hair to grow in plaits of length even longer than his lengthy grey-white beard. He occasionally wore a green coat, later a red tartan shawl, which covered his bright waistcoat with its two rows of brass buttons, each embossed with a goat. These were specially made sets, one showing a billy-goat standing, another a nanny-goat laying down and a third showing a standing kid.

His spotless linen blouse, the collars and cuffs scalloped and hand-stitched in semi-circular pattern, were worn outside his green trousers, made of elegant facecloth and livened with a narrow red silk braid cut in Vandyke fashion around the edge. In later years, he said this was a uniform worn by Welshmen when they defeated the English at the Battle of Bosworth Field.

He claimed that Dr Coch, who carried the Red Dragon at the battle, was his ancestor. Dr Coch was an authentic person, namely Dr Ellis Price of Plas Iolyn, whose grandfather, Rhys Fawr, did in fact act as standard bearer at Bosworth on August 12, 1485.

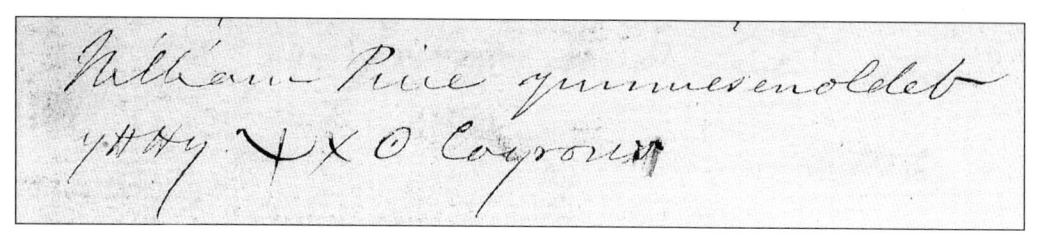

The signature – complete with Druidic lettering – adopted by Dr Price.

During one of his many court hearings, the *Cardiff and Merthyr Guardian* appeared to take more interest in his outfit than in the actual case. One report read, "This eccentric gentleman is a son of a deceased clergyman who wears a beard flowing down to his waist and his hair, which has evidently not been cut for years, is of equal length and is tied up in sundry tails like the Chinese.

"His dress consists of a jacket and trousers of emerald green fancifully notched and scalloped, lined and pointed in bright scarlet and adorned with numerous small gilt buttons bearing the image of goats. His cap is of sable, equally quaint, and has attached three tails of fur, one falling over each shoulder and the third hanging down the centre of his back."

Around the same period, he began to place what many thought were medical honours after his name, such as VSLM. In fact, they were anything but, for the series of letters made a strange mixture of Welsh and French in "Fi si li mer" or "I am the flood of the ocean", again referring to Druidic lore.

His title in the Medical Directory of 1886 actually read: "PRICE, William, V.S.L.M., Llantrissent, Glamorganch. M.R.C.S., Eng, A.L.S.A. 1821 (St Barthol. A Lond. Hosp.). Decipher of "Gwyllllis yn Nayd". Discoverer of Gavval Lenn Berren Myurrdhdhin Syllt Tyurn wiallen Cyur Aneurin Gwawtrudh Awennudh Privv Varrydh Nuadh y Brann Gwunn Gwislen Lsnn ab Lann ab Deyl ap Peyl Sarrph ynus Pruttan a ych Chyoul Brenn Privv Varrydh Dusce Cymmru a Gwylllis yn Nayd."

This astonishing and incomprehensible entry was improved the following year with the addition of "Author of Pedigree of Iesu Grist". Dr Price explained that the entry recorded not only his medical qualifications, "but also his Druidical discoveries".

On his return to Wales in July 1840, it was obvious the Marquis of Bute maintained a watchful eye on the surgeon and the local constabulary took extra precautions that he was not conducting political meetings in Upper Boat and Pontypridd, as was presumed. He continued working for Crawshay and resumed involvement with Chartism. In June 1840, an attempt was made to assassinate Queen Victoria and meetings all over the country responded by declaring their loyalty to her and congratulating Her Majesty on her survival. Not in Pontypridd. When the local gentlemen and clergy arrived at the hall, Price and his friends were already in occupation. The "respectables" proposed the chair should be taken by the Rev David Williams of the new St Mary's Church, Glyntaff. Price proposed William Williams, landlord of the Prince of Wales beerhouse. Price won the vote and the "respectables" adjourned to another room to vote their loyalty without interference.

Police Constable Phil Banner gave information of meetings held by Price in Newbridge every Sunday, when his friends paraded around with walking sticks shaped like bayonets and covered in Druidic symbols. "The house belongs to Thomas Morgan, cabinet-maker; the number who attend are usually fourteen or fifteen. They are all violent and notorious Chartists and are called 'Mr Price's Scholars.'"

Dr John Cule explained, "By the end of 1840 the Chartists had diminished and appeared to have little influence over workers in the area. Though in company with other Chartists, Dr Price was quieter, he was by no means cowed and when in January 1841 Richard Jones, weaver of Llanrwst, was charged with distributing seditious publications in Newbridge, Mr Price, surgeon, of Newbridge, a gentleman well known for his predilection for the Chartist cause, offered himself as a surety in ten pounds, with Thomas Morgan, carpenter of the same place.

"Richard Jones himself was referred to in the newspaper account as "this dirty Demosthenes", but he proudly claimed that he was "only accountable to God for his actions."

During the general election of 1841, significant political divisions developed in the Chartist movement, both nationally and locally. The Monmouthshire Chartists were divided over the question of what attitude to adopt towards the two political parties in Parliament – the Whigs and the Tories. On the day of the nomination, William Edwards, the baker and founder of the Newport Working Men's Association, was nominated as the Chartist candidate. He was a supporter of the Whig promises of reform and advocated giving them a second chance. But the meeting was then thrown into confusion by the entrance of Dr Price, who was also proposed as a candidate. Price's nomination was not accepted. Edwards won the show of hands and then withdrew from the poll. This caused uproar, with many regarding Edwards's withdrawal as a betrayal. Price continued to be involved in the movement for some time to come, but did not appear to involve himself in the next phase of the Chartism in 1848.

He complained of a wholesaler's boycott of the Pontypridd Co-operative in 1841. The store seems to have survived the crisis, for when the Newbridge chain workers struck against a reduction in wages in April 1842, he was able to supply them with a large amount of provisions. With a working-class movement in disarray and a popular national culture initially under heavy attack, Price, the Welsh rebel, turned to individual protest and Druidic fantasy on a grand scale.

Faced with a situation in which he saw the culture of his people under attack and their history denied, he reacted by reaffirming, through invention, their existence as Iolo Morganwg had done years before. While he created material of his own, not quite forging a national consciousness as Iolo had done, there was another public arena of which he could play a major part. It was time for him to enter the law courts.

Chapter Six
THE LITIGANT

WILLIAM Price was a well known figure in the courts of law where, dressed in one of his typically flamboyant uniforms, he relentlessly turned his energies to litigation. Blunt and forthright, he had nothing but contempt for the English legal system but was often found in court, enjoying every moment of the proceedings and, always the showman, shamelessly playing to the gallery. Also, he proved an awkward litigant and one particular case was temporarily halted because he refused to swear on the Bible.

He argued that he could not vouch for the accuracy of the map of Judea in it and when a second Bible arrived, failed to vouch for the accuracy of the name of the owner on the inside cover. Everyone looked forward to a Price court case. It became his favourite pastime and he believed his involvement in the courts added to his stature.

Litigation is frequently associated with schizophrenia and in it Dr Price may have found the means of expressing his paranoia. Here he had his audience to play to, an arena where he was the central character – a character away from his life as a surgeon. Generally, people accepted him in a rigid Victorian era because of his outstanding success as a healer. On one hand they were afraid or at least somewhat sceptical of his peculiarities as a self-confessed Druid, but as a physician, their trust in him remained unwavering. Now he wanted to challenge a new, higher social class by entering the courtroom and displaying his total defiance and contempt of them publicly.

His unconventional mode of living and his heretical beliefs had already aroused a fury and hatred of the preachers and other pillars of respectability. Gossip, pulpit and press were used to spread stories about him. The preachers of his time invented the first Welsh atrocity with the idea of discrediting him in the eyes of the "faithful".

Having exhumed the body of his father during the proceedings of one particular court case, they seized upon the incident to give vent to their hatred and spite by saying that he cut the head off. The event came about as a result of a court case held in Bristol in 1848 to decide whether Dr Price's father had been insane in 1809 when he sold 85 acres of land in the Rudry area. The reverend died in 1841.

The defendants were the Trustees of the Children of the Fothergill family, later owners of Hensol Castle, who had bought the property from his father. Quite simply, Dr Price wanted the land returned to him. Numerous witnesses testified that the Rev Price was undoubtedly insane for the last forty years of his life. Indeed, the signing of the necessary documents in 1809 was delayed for a day because the Rev Price had inadvertently jumped out of a window. The estate was in equity for fifteen years and it became necessary in the course of the proceedings to prove the father had been incompetent for many years to manage the estate and had no right to have sold the land.

Price explained that his father had a fall in his youth "which left him helpless at times". The post mortem could not prove a mental illness, although the doctor claimed that the vessels of his father's brain were unduly large. It was carried out in the presence of Dr Edwards of Caerphilly and Dr Davies of Bedwas, under the direction of the Court of Chancery. The event did nothing to endear Price to his neighbours, who embellished the story further with tales of dreadful Druidic rites of grave desecration. Lord Chancellor Cotton, who tried the case, was very much in Price's favour, and gave him the verdict, but it was refused on appeal and Price claimed to have lost £4,000.

Later, he tried to re-establish the family fortune by placing a claim to the Ruperra Estate, lands that included Monmouth and Brecon and were owned by the Barons of Tredegar, which he referred to the High Court. Dr Price claimed it had always belonged to the Druids, and Hugh Jones of Machen, a person who was accredited by Price with the ownership of the estate, had bequeathed it by Will to his father when he was a young man. His father, by reason of his mental illness, had allowed it to lapse.

Dr Price went on to explain in his interview: "My father was a Druid, baptised in Gellywastad House in Machen by Hugh Jones. This was the only place where the Druids baptised their sons, and on a gravestone in Machen parish churchyard you will find a very big coat of arms with an oblong concave dish which held the water at the ceremony of baptism.

"It is funny, I can read the arms of the Druids, and no one who is not an Archdruid can do that. Hugh Jones, I should tell you, was the owner of the Ruperra Estate, which always belonged to the Druids.

"The owner of Ruperra was supposed to possess a power inherent in him to baptise, and could bequeath the property to whom he pleased. Hugh Jones in his Will bequeathed Ruperra to my father and appointed John Morgan, a Druid, of Tredegar, as executor.

"Hugh Jones lent John Morgan £40,000 to take possession of Tredegar. My father was 13 years old at the time when Jones died in 1777, but because of a fall my father had upon his head he was incompetent in keeping the property. I have deposited in the Public Record Office in London an affidavit of 725 folios, in which I trace my right to Ruperra, and have exhibited 120 proofs that I claim the authority that the Primitive Bard had to govern the world.

"I proved my claim to it, but judgement was given against me. I intend to bring another action to recover Ruperra. I have traced several important facts on a stone in the hamlet of Llanbedr and I exhibited the stone itself in the proofs I speak of. Llanbedr means Church of Baptism and no one but a Druid has the right to baptise."

On taking up the case, Price attempted to affirm his lineal, Druidic descent and argued he was able to read the inscriptions of the Druids, a unique gift which he believed made him an Archdruid, but nothing came of it.

Hiarlles and Dr William Price

Forever denouncing lawyers, he once charged an assistant bailiff to the County Court at Cardiff, Frederick Burns, with owing him 10d, but when the judge examined the documents he found that an error of 6d only had been made and ordered a repayment.

On another occasion, he accused officers of the County Court with having planned a conspiracy against his reputation, because he had exposed an act of extortion committed by the Judge's "satellites, Robert Langley, Frederick Burns and others in the Queen's name, under the Seal of Court, by putting an execution into my house on the 1st of December 1852 and plundering therefrom the sum of £5 11s 4d which had been paid once by me before, as the receipt proves."

However, there was obviously a busy life to lead outside of the courthouse. According to varying reports, Dr Price – a firm advocator of free love - fathered his first child in 1841, with an Ann Morgan of Pentyrch, with whom he remained until her death in 1866. Sadly for Price, it was not the son he had hoped for and therefore not the Druidic messiah proclaimed in the song of the primitive bard.

Astonishingly, the child was named Gwenhiolen Hiarlles Morganwg (Gwenllian Iarlles Morganwg or Gwenllian, Countess of Glamorgan). He claimed that she deserved the grand title by right of her distinguished descendancy from the Prince of Wales.

He baptised her in a peculiar Druidic ceremony at the Rocking Stone and signed the birth certificate himself with unintelligible hieroglyphics. It was a signature he used frequently, although not always as Dr William Price, sometimes as Arglwydd Rhys of Deheubarth.

In later years, he began to refer to himself and his daughter as the Children of the Lord Rhys, leader of the rising against the English in 1165. On another occasion, they became children of Owain Llawgoch (Owen of the Red Hand), who fought with the French against Edward III and passed into Welsh legend as a hero who would one day return to rule over Britain. Despite his obsession with having a god-like son, for now, it was Hiarlles who was his only known offspring and when she was barely four years old, he belittled the majesty of the law by insisting the child was his assistant in a court case, naming her "my learned counsel."

Gwenhiolen Hiarlles Morganwg pictured in c.1870

In 1846, Dr Price suffered a burglary at his home, when he found that his cupboard drawers had been broken into and £70.00 stolen from his waistcoat pocket. He had then in his employ a housekeeper who had been with him some time, and a new maidservant called Jennett Lewis. Price suspected Jennett and had her arrested. But when she came to be examined at Cardiff and Caerphilly, it seemed to the magistrates that the other servant was the more likely culprit.

The case was dismissed for lack of evidence. Price, smarting under his loss, refused to pay her wages. The girl then brought an action demanding her wages, but Price was determined not to pay her. After the examination of her mother, he asked for an adjournment, saying, in his defence, that he was now able to bring further evidence against her and would spend £50.00 on the prosecution. At the close of the proceedings, Price distributed copies of the depositions in Welsh.

There was a further hearing of the case in June 1847 before Mr Wilson, Judge of the Circuit, in the Small Debts Court. The claim of the servant was for 7s 10d and Price counter claimed she robbed him of £69 10s.

The judge, after hearing the witnesses, decided the charge could not be sustained, and an order for payment was made against Price, which he discharged.

On February 8, 1848, at Merthyr County Court, Price brought an action against his fellow practitioner, David Gwynne Owen, to recover the sum of £20.00. In the summer of 1847, both had been practising in partnership at Llanfabon, but Dr Owen was living in retirement in Monmouth. It appeared that it was their custom not to include receipts from private patients in the partnership accounts. Price had a private patient whom Owen had been called to attend. After the dissolution of the partnership, Owen found the leaves of these entries had been torn from the book and felt that he was owed £150 by Price. No further court reports can be found.

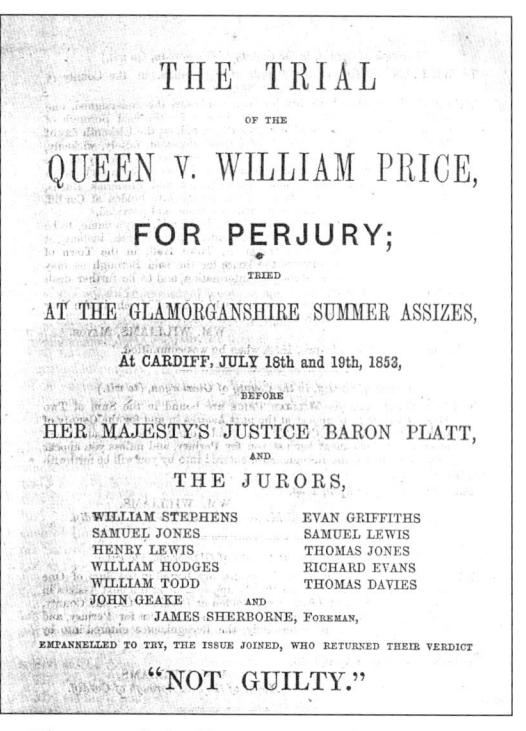

The cover of a booklet containing the proceedings of the Trial, 1853.

At the time, Price was made surgeon at Gellygaer Colliery and J.C. Maddever, a former assistant to Mr Owen, had become his assistant, also. In July 1848, Maddever made a successful claim against Price for his wages of 25s per week. In February 1850, Price brought an action against James Curtis, a relative of William Watson of the Castle Inn, Treforest, to recover compensation by way of damages for an assault committed near Pwll Nant y Dedd in Pontypridd on January 15. Damages were laid at £5.00. Price conducted his own defence. The judge eventually ordered 10s damages, with full costs.

Dr Price was also known for causing added confusion to a court hearing by using his brother's name instead of his own. It was well illustrated in an encounter at the Cardiff Small Debts Court on June 12, 1850, before Judge John Wilson. Miss Maria Price, of Cardiff, attempted to recover from the doctor the possession of a piece of land of 45 acres called Mynyddybwlch in Rudry. Price had coveted this property in 1838 to graze his young cattle. The land, however, was already let and the doctor persuaded Miss Price to transfer tenancy to him.

This seemed a simple situation, but to recover the land she had to take it to court. To make the situation worse, Dr Price succeeded in getting the matter referred to the Court of the Queen's Bench. It appeared that when Price fled to France, his brother Charles managed his affairs and his name appeared on the rate book.

But the rent had not been paid for five years and when a certain Robert Williams attempted to serve notice on the doctor, he locked him in the surgery until he agreed to serve the notice on his brother. The case excited considerable interest, particularly when the judge ruled that it was Charles Price upon whom she should have served notice.

Dr Price was later involved with a famous trial on July 18 and 19, 1853, when he was indicted for perjury at the Glamorgan Assizes, before Justice Baron Platt. It was due to publishing a printer's pamphlet of forty pages, containing a transcript of the shorthand notes of the evidence given at a previous trial. Held at Cardiff, due to an Ann Millward who extorted money from her brother William, Price was accused of prompting Millward to exact the money and found himself back in court for perjury.

Hiarlles, the doctor's first child, born in 1841.

He even published the entire legal encounter called "The Trial versus William Price", which was privately printed by William Hemmons of Broad Street, Bristol and sold for 6d per copy. Price again conducted his own defence with young Hiarlles, who was accommodated with a seat at the barristers' table. To cause further chaos during the trial, he had challenged a large number of jurymen, refused to swear on the Bible, and eventually swore on a Testament and left the whole court agape with astonishment.

His speech opened, "As my brain has been ploughed and harrowed for the last five months, and sown by the conspirators with the seeds of villainy and malice, I beg you to listen to me patiently and with all the indulgence you can afford, while I, an innocent victim of persecution, mow down their harvest of perjury!

"I think that I shall be able to prove to your satisfaction that this charge of perjury against me was born and bred in the brain of Judge Thomas Falconer, and nourished by his sinister influence over the conspirators, John Bird, Robert Langley, Frederick Burns, John Hodkinson, and other greater and lesser lights in the background plot, for the express purpose of taking away my liberty, destroying my reputation, and arresting my right course, because I have repeatedly refused to prostrate my senses in this Court and other places at his dictates and their threatenings of prosecution.

"Cannot her Majesty, as the mighty huntress, in her day, before the Lord, go out like the Sun, to find beasts of prey enough for her bloodhounds without hunting them to sacrifice the liberty and the life of an innocent man upon her criminal altars with the bloody hands of her priesthood?

"What! Does the equivalent Queen of Great Britain, the mistress of the civilised world, in her day, fear the light of the Sun, living in a drop of dew, and identified in the name of William Price? Observe the common animus of this prosecution for innocent blood, as well as the blood of the innocent, in the name of the Queen of Great Britain. These are the facts, the circumstances and connection of the events on which this villainous ex-officio prosecution is based, and the extreme questions I have asked are necessary for a correct solution."I submit them to your serious consideration, and to be answered by your verdict. My blood, my liberty, and my life are in your custody this day. I ask you to do me justice. The villainy, conspiracy, and malice of my prosecutors thirsting for my blood have sworn me guilty by perjuring themselves. Truth, justice and common sense say 'no, no'.

"There is no foundation for it. Not guilty! Remember that my fate is sealed by the word of your mouth. Your will be done on earth as it is in heaven."

Following a 16-hour-long day in the courtroom, the jury deliberated for just twenty minutes and he was found not guilty. When the trial closed at 1.15am, he was greeted by a massive applause in the public gallery and on the street.

Gradually, he began to withdraw from any further legal skirmishes from 1858 onwards until the infamous trial of 1884, illustrating something of a withdrawal from the public arena into an even deeper world of his own fantastic creation.

Chapter Seven

THE WELSHMAN

THE mental state of Dr William Price must surely have been brought into question by the time he reached middle age. In 1851, he visited the International Exhibition in Cardiff in a goat-drawn carriage, such was his love for the animal. Price had goats and sheep immortalised in a serious of paintings at his home and his proudest possession was his Glamorgan herd of cattle, which he specifically disposed of in his will.

However, as a Welshman, he obviously tried his utmost to defend his people and their heritage to the best of his ability. He summoned the champions of the Welsh past to fight the enemy of the present – the capitalist class. At the height of the British Empire, he fought when the battle could not be won. The small, Welsh nation was powerless against the might of the Empire. His mind could not withstand the terrible pressures of defeat, but he stayed at his post when few others did. That is why he is remembered with such affection and respect.

Although he never completely lost touch with reality, his Druidic fantasies became progressively more extreme and extravagant. In 1844, his attempt to organise an eisteddfod in Pontypridd was a dismal failure. No one entered the competition and the only event of note seems to have been the initiation of two-year-old Hiarlles. The event took place only shortly after the death of his mother, Mary, on January 5, aged 77.

In 1855, the editor of the *Cardiff and Merthyr Guardian* voiced his absolute disgust at the conduct of an eisteddfod held in Merthyr Tydfil. The Ivorites, or the Welsh Language Friendly Society, held a procession through the streets to Tabernacle Chapel. They were led by three individuals - Price in full costume, a half-naked Aberdare man called Myrddin, covered in dark paint and wearing a white animal skin over his shoulder, and a goat.

Dr William Price in full Druidic costume c.1870.

It was not totally unlike the procession of the Welsh Regiment's Goat Major at the Crimea a year later. According to the report, the goat was the most respectable and best behaved of the three. On arrival at the chapel, they were welcomed into the eisteddfod.

In 1861, he sent the following strange notice to a local printer to produce copies: "All the Greek Books are the Works of the Primitive Bards, in our own Language!!!!!! There is a Discovery for the Cymmerian Race!!!!! Discovered by me in 1839!!!! No man living can form an opinion, or imagine, the consequence of my Discovery. Before he shall be taught, by me, to read Homer, The Greek New Testament, or any and all The Greek Classics, which I can do, perfectly, in less than six days!!!!! Homer was born in the Hamlet of Y Van near Caerphili. He built Caerphili Castle... the oldest Books of the Chinese confess the Fact!! This look more like a dream than a Reality in the absence of light".

Price asked the printer to produce the notice under the title 'Plant Owein Lawgoch' (The Children of Owain Llawgoch) in red ink and went on to create his own strange mythology based on historical figures and his own ideas on Druidism. His actions enjoyed something of an uncanny likeness to the eccentricities of Iolo Morganwg.

Price, of course, was the most colourful of a number of individuals who tended in the same direction – towards a pyrotechnic combination of political radicalism, historical forgery and Druidic mythology. It comes as little surprise that Dr Price felt such an affinity with Iolo, particularly this ever-increasing obsession with Druidism. Such was Price's passion for the religion, he went on to build the famous Round Houses at Craig yr Helfa, Glyntaf in 1860, complete with a symbol of the letter 'T' on the top of the dome, being the Cymmerian pre-Christian cross. They were to be his museum to Druidism, a school for poor children and reminiscent of the centre he envisaged on the site of the Rocking Stones, twenty years earlier. The Round Houses were to be the opening gates to the main building, which never materialised due to lack of funds and a disagreement with the landowner who was Lady Llanover, no less. A giant of Welsh culture, Lady Llanover was undoubtedly, one of the most hugely influential and colourful characters of 19th century Wales.

She was the force behind recreating a new national pride for a country, condemned by Her Majesty's 1847 Blue Books inspection. The Welsh psyche hit rock bottom, but it was the likes of Llanover and her close friend, Charlotte Guest, who began a process of rebuilding national pride. Lady Llanover (Augusta Waddington) was born in 1802 and, in 1823, she married Benjamin Hall III, of Abercarn, later to become a local MP who was elevated to the peerage in 1859.

He is best remembered for having been Commissioner for Works in 1855, when the clock on the Houses of Parliament was built – the bell being named "Big Ben". Hall was a tall, imposing man, and was probably the source of the naming of the bell.

The Round Houses at Glyntaff, Pontypridd

It was the unity of such vast Llanover and Abercarn estates that saw the Halls become the most influential couple in Wales. They shared a dream to build a house which would become a centre for Welsh culture. It was a place where bards, musicians, historians and academics could come to study, exchange views, and enjoy the society of like-minded people. In fact, they were almost obsessive in their dream, one not so far from the hopes and aspirations of Dr Price himself. Lady Llanover, in an effort to create a new identity for the Welsh people to the rest of the world, influenced the wearing of a "national dress" of Welsh flannel, based on clothing worn by countrywomen during the early 19th century. The tall hat did not appear until the late 1840s.

The elderly Hiarlles Morganwg pictured in later life at East Caerlan, Llantrisant, with Gwenllian.

They held ten eisteddfodau between 1834 and 1853, each one more magnificent than its predecessor. The prizes were enormous, and competitors came from all corners of the globe, including Karl Meyer and Albert Schultz, from Germany. She even assisted Lady Charlotte Guest in translating the Mabinogion before her death in 1896, at the age of 92.

Price's involvement with the Llanover dynasty showed signs of deterioration in 1859, when he was ordered to sell a portion of his land for the building of a railway to a local colliery working with the Treforest Tramway Company. Price refused to give up the land, and in consequence, the Llanovers, who owned the coal mining area, sought damages against him. The land had some complicated history.

On 5 March, 1853, Sir Benjamin Hall leased to Price the building ground which was part of the Pentrebach lands for 21 years at the sum of £20 per annum. Sir Benjamin reserved the mineral rights on the land and Price was allowed to build "one good substantial dwelling house" there.

At first, Price and Llanover appeared on friendly terms. They both enjoyed an incredible enthusiasm for Welsh culture and heritage, but Price's eccentricities seem to have appeared too bewildering for the aristocrat. Work on excavating the site at Glyntaf began with the building of the Round Houses, but in 1861, Lady Llanover insisted on evicting him, with heavy costs, particularly to the unpaid builders who supplied the material. Dr Price refused to pay and a warrant was issued. His home was surrounded by police and Hiarlles suggested he should hide in an old chest.

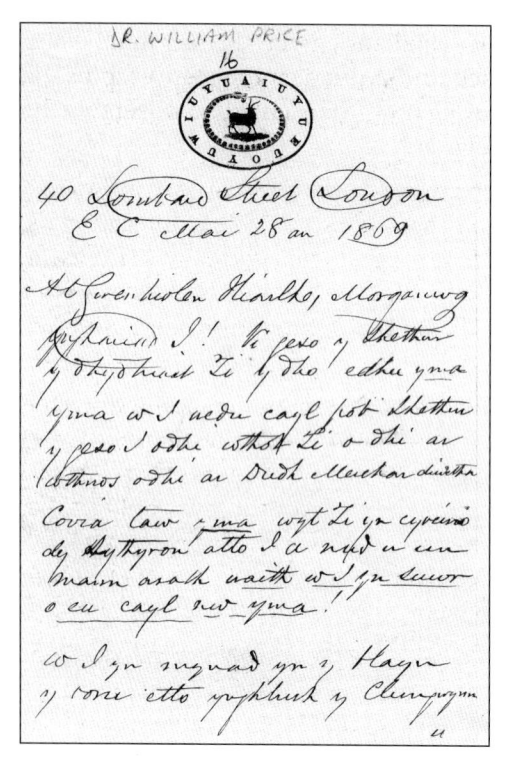

Price scrambled inside and she locked him in so the police could find no sign of him. Later that day, the trunk was allegedly carried out of the house by two friends, claiming it contained clothing. Whether the local constabulary were really that naive is hard to imagine!

Declared bankrupt, he again escaped to Paris, pending an appeal which proved successful, ordering him to pay £2,000 damages to the railway company. His letter, written at the Great Western Hotel, Paddington, London, in January 1861 to Hiarlles talks of the authorities as the "devil closing in on him", but he goes on to say "ond yr wyf yn meddwl yr af trwyddo" (I think I will get through) and signs it "Dy Dad" (your father) William Price." He also suggests her mother, Ann Morgan, goes to stay with the "ladies" at Trallwn, until his exile is over.

A letter from the doctor to Hiarlles in 1869 (notice his personal notepaper).

While in Paris on his second exile, which supposedly lasted six years, he met Pierre Joseph Proudhon (1809-1865), French philosopher and social theorist who had a massive effect on the post-1848 revolutionary France.

According to the Welshman, Price still enjoyed many love affairs, particularly with a certain Madame Bisset.

In June 1866, he returned to Wales, settling once more in Pontypridd before eventually moving to the historic hilltop market town of Llantrisant in about 1871.

Precisely why he decided to move after more than forty years in Pontypridd is uncertain, particularly since Llantrisant had begun to decline with the loss of its regular markets and fairs.

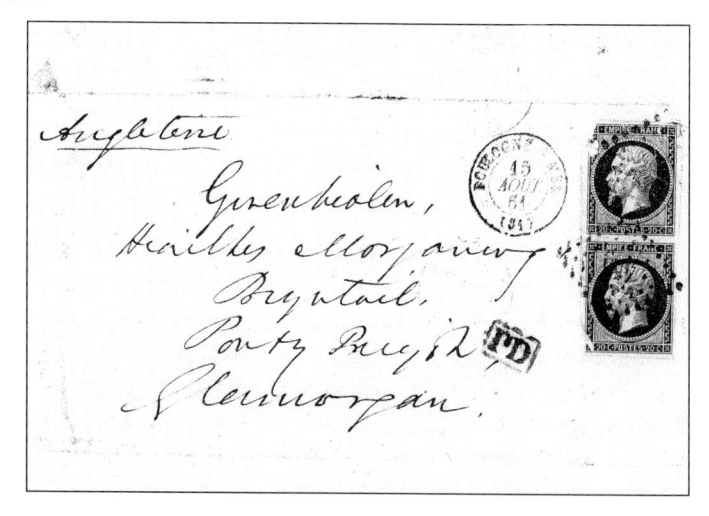

The envelope, dated 1869, to Hiarlles

74

However, his partner Ann Morgan had since died and, given the fact that he had departed from Pontypridd to France under such undignified circumstances, plus the fact that his dream of a museum and home at Glyntaff had failed so miserably, he may have felt the time was right to move elsewhere.

The medieval market town of Llantrisant provided a perfect hamlet for the doctor, who retired as surgeon of the Brown Lenox chainworks in 1871 at the age of 71. In the same year, he was to lose his brother, Charles, at the age of 80, who lived the last few years of his life in Caeridwen, near Radyr. In the following year, his other sister, Elizabeth, died at 9.20am on October 25, 1872 at Pentwyn, Rudry, and was buried four days later at Bedwas.

Commanding an outstanding setting on the crest of a hill and enjoying the most picturesque surrounding landscape, historic Llantrisant was one of the most celebrated ancient towns in Wales. The eminence of such a magnificent hilltop fortress town was crowned by its medieval Norman castle, once used as an overnight prison for King Edward II, and a fine parish church surrounded by a cluster of homes scattered throughout its charming, unplanned cobbled streets. Surrounded by lush green landscape and steeped in history, it also enjoyed an air of eccentricity about it.

Price revelled in his new hometown, although little is known of his involvement in Llantrisant's many activities. He didn't appear to involve himself in many of the traditions associated with the town, such as the Beating the Bounds ceremony which was held every seven years by the ancient order of the Freemen. Hundreds would walk the seven-mile boundary of the ancient borough of Llantrisant to exercise their rights over the common lands. However, Price used those lands extensively for his many, long walks, usually naked. Similarly, knowing Price's total disregard for authority, he would hardly have immersed himself in the local celebrations when a farmer's son, David Evans, became Lord Mayor of London and paraded through the streets of the old town in 1892, lined with well-wishers.

Undoubtedly, he ridiculed the chapel-goers, dismissed the church folk, too, but enjoyed the many facilities at the local public houses – those who served him cider, or better still champagne, at least. In 1871, an incredible 27 pubs existed in the hilltop town itself. One of his closest friends was Roderick Lewis, landlord of the Wheatsheaf Hotel. In one particular incident, while escaping an angry mob, he hid in the Bear Inn on the Bull Ring and even planned out a cremation at the Cross Keys, prior to ascending Caerlan fields with the body of his son.

Dr Price's new home was Ty'r Clettwr, situated on the bend of the High Street from Southgate, where he remained for the next 25 years and continued to practise as a surgeon. The community were understandably concerned about their new neighbour. He also invested in a great deal of land and property in the district, purchasing fields at East Caerlan by 1873. Few could ignore his handsome presence, dominant character, romantic costume and theories, which attracted the eye of the ladies. They were deliciously alarmed by him and his views on marriage. Obviously, the women of the parish were somewhat in awe of this figure in their midst. Many failed to resist his advances.

Llantrisant, as portrayed by H. Gastineau c.1823.

According to his letters, he often travelled to North Wales and learned about bone-setting and the manipulation of bones by therapist Evan Davies. Through Davies, he also met Hugh Owen Thomas of Liverpool, with whom he corresponded for years. Thomas created the bed knee splint, widely used on troops in the First World War.

However, it is clear that his fantasies were becoming all the more extreme with old age and there were undoubtedly lapses in his behaviour, although not nearly as severe as those suffered by his late father.

In June 1871, the coalminers of Aberdare and Rhondda came out on strike for a five percent increase in wages. It was a bitter 12-week period in the South Wales coalfield, which resulted in the establishment of a miners' union, the Amalgamated Association of Miners.

Dr Price took their cause to his heart, openly condemning the local mineowners as "Welsh Pharaohs". His opening speech about the owners to the Aberdare miners was impressive to say the least, and not overpowered with the ramblings one had come to expect. Filled with passion, it was clear, confident, direct and, most of all, inspiring: "You are the Welsh Pharaohs who think you can suck the lifeblood of the colliers for ever. You have grown fat and prosperous, you own the big houses, you wear the finest clothes, your children are healthy and happy, yet you do not work. How, then, have you got these things by idleness? Let me tell you. You have been stealing the balance of the low wages which you have been paying them. Take heed you men whose bodies and souls are bloated by the lifeblood of the poor, take heed before it is too late. Remember that the oppression of the Pharaohs of Egypt did not last for ever, and neither will the blood-sucking Pharaohs of Wales."

In the local press, a writer named "Belted Will" wrote articles against Dr Price, endeavouring to prejudice the miners against him. Price retaliated with the following announcement:

"To the Sane and Peaceful Colliers of the Aberdare and Rhondda Valleys, lately on Strike against their Pharaohs:

> *"Strange that such Difference should be*
> *Tween wheedle you and wheedle me!*
> *And Stranger still that Belted Will*
> *With O – M – 's hand and Quill!*
> *Should analyse his "BC" Bubble!*
> *To save the Doctor's Ink and Trouble!*
> *Save me? No! You twaddling donkey!*
> *Balamm's Ass is not so empty!"*

By William Price – In the Presence of the Sun at Ponty y Priyth, November 1 1871.

Gwenllian Llewellyn (1859-1948).

In 1873, he was acquitted of the manslaughter of a patient named Thomas Price of Penydarren, Merthyr, who consulted him on the swelling on his knee. He told the court, "I commanded him to remain in bed, and forbade him to leave his house, but, notwithstanding, he, one day, in company with his brother and others, drove in a trap to Pontypridd to see me.

"He was carried by them into the surgery, but, after I had taken out an accumulation of matter from his knee, he was able to walk about unaided. It was then about five o'clock in the evening, and I instructed the man to go home at once, and not to delay on the road, so as to be home before dark. In fact, I offered him a bed at The Duke.

"Instead of obeying my commands, he and his friends called at several public houses on the road, and it was four or five o'clock in the morning before he reached home. The result was the poor fellow caught cold, which developed into inflammation of the lungs, and ultimately he died."

Price demanded the body be exhumed. Three medical men from Merthyr swore the deceased had been maltreated by Price and he had caused the death. A verdict of manslaughter was passed. Under the authority of Mr Austin Bruce, later Lord Aberdare and Home Secretary for a time, the body was exhumed and a post mortem held in Vaynor Church, with Dr John James of Merthyr in attendance.

The results proved he died of lung disease. Despite the finding, the trial for manslaughter took place at Swansea Assizes. Dr Price later explained, "Dr Dyke of Merthyr was a prominent witness against me, but Dr James and Dr Davies of Bedwas, who conducted the post mortem examination, gave evidence on my behalf. I conducted my own defence, and the jury, of course, returned a verdict of 'not guilty'".

In February 1874, Shakespeare's *Othello* was produced under Price's patronage in the Market Place of Pontypridd by the Welsh Model Theatre. A somewhat unlikely tale of Price's life is the visit he made in 1875 to a medical conference in London. According to Price, he went to a Soho pub and met his old friend Cledwyn Hughes, who allegedly introduced him to none other than the revolutionary Karl Marx, father of the Communist Manifesto.

In 1879, he visited his relatives' graves at Bedwas Church to find excavations were being carried out in the chancel. Human bones had been taken from the chancel for reburial in the churchyard and Price picked up a piece and claimed it was a bone from his sister. He accused the rector, Rev William Williams, of sacrilege, and later erected a brass plate on the Price family tomb, bearing a verse which chastised the clergyman for removing the remains. The plate remained there until April 1967 when, green with age, it mysteriously disappeared.

Sometime during the late 1870s, he met Gwenllian Llewellyn of Llanwynno. It is believed she visited him at his surgery in Llantrisant and he was besotted with her, claiming "Isis has come, the Mother of Gods has visited my habitation! Her forehead is high like that of the Goddess Juno, and her brow is like that of the Goddess Minerva!"

She was born at Cwm Eldeg in Cilfynydd on 23 October, 1859. Her family were the Llewellyns of Llanwonno, and originally farmed at Ynys-cae-dudwg, later the site of the Albion Colliery. Her mother, grandmother and their maidservant all died of typhoid fever. The manservant took fright and disappeared. At this time, Gwen was only 12 years of age and the remainder of her family moved to farm at Coed y Goran, St Mellons.

Her father died when she was 16, and she was sent to her aunt at Llanharan, where she met Dr Price. Apparently, a form of "Druidic marriage" took place between them at the Rocking Stone on the doctor's 81st birthday in March 1881. Gwenllian was just 21. In Gwenllian he saw his ideal partner, someone who understood his Druidic leanings and was prepared to accept his often peculiar behaviour, also someone young enough to bear his children. The housekeeper moved to Ty'r Clettwr, understandably causing a stir in the close-knit community of Llantrisant, although she remained in the town for the next 60 years.

The Census of 1881 names Ty'r Clettwr as Pen Ty Cae Cledar, listing the occupants as 81-year-old Dr Price, with Gwenllian as his 21-year-old daughter, and a 20-year-old servant named Margaret Griffiths. Ten years later and the Census names Gwenllian as a 31-year-old housekeeper with two children. Under the column for the number of languages spoken, they all say "both", meaning English and Welsh.

During the late 1870s and early 1880s, he continued to play a very active role in the many ceremonies held at the Rocking Stone. The *Western Mail* is littered with accounts of his visits to the market town to attend the Meeting of the Bards on the occasion of an equinox.

The newspaper account for March 23, 1881 reads: "Extraordinary scene on Pontypridd Common. On Monday at noon, the actual day of the Vernal Equinox, an apparition appeared in the streets of Treforest. It was robed in white. On its head was the whole skin of the Anubis of the Egyptian priests of Osiris. Its nether garment was a commonplace article called a trouser, lined with red. From a wand resting on the shoulder streamed a large flag of crimson silk. The bearer was Dr William Price.

"The whole town were at their doors and many followed the strange visitors. Having reached the rocking stone the doctor mounted it exactly at noon and addressed the sun he proceeded to speak in the strange Welsh, it was supposed, of the pre-Adamite epoch. The audience was in convulsions of laughter, but not a smile was on the performer's face."

Only a few months later, he appeared at the site once more for the feast of Alban Hefin and wore a suit of light grey, home-made Welsh cloth and on his head a white hat. Indeed, they laughed at his behaviour and his Druidic beliefs, but shortly this lighthearted mockery would turn into sheer disgust and horror.

Chapter Eight

The Heretic

DREAMS of a godlike-son were answered on 8 August, 1883, when Gwenllian gave birth to a baby boy. Following his prophecy, Dr Price called the child Iesu Grist (Jesus Christ). The child was centred on all his hopes and aspirations, claiming his birth and functions had been foretold from ancient days. The baby was the fulfilment of his life, and would restore the lost secrets of the Druids. He claimed the right to call his child Iesu Grist came from Gwyllllis yn Nayd, the prophecy which foresaw the birth.

In ancient times, the governor or king of the country was always selected by the Druids, and the person they selected was called Mab Duw, The Son of God. As Price later explained:

"It was for this reason that Cynddelw called Llewellyn, the second Welsh prince of that name, by the title. I have proof positive that I am the son of the Welsh Primitive Bard and I am equally certain that this second child of mine, who I have also called Iesu Grist, will reign on earth, and that in him the ancient Druidical system will be restored."

How utterly incredible was the fact that Dr Price was confusing Christianity with Druidism here. Admittedly, earlier Christian history had adopted pagan ceremonies into its own, but for Price – a man totally opposed to modern religion – to name his son Iesu Grist seems quite absurd. Although he explained the child would be the Son of God, obviously he was referring to the Druidic gods, not that of Christianity. One wonders whether in naming the baby Jesus, or Iesu in Welsh, he was either mocking the Christian church and chapel which held such power in Victorian Wales, or it was quite simply down to his confused mind.

It is said the baby had strange marks on his back, one that even resembled a man on horseback that first appeared when he was only three weeks old. Ill health plagued the baby until, tragically, Iesu died after only five months in its cradle in the front room of Ty'r Clettwr on January 10, 1884, but in doing so, secured his father's place in history.

Cremation was another of Price's passionate interests, and he advocated it frequently in accordance with the ancient practices of the Druids, who also burned their dead. It was not practised in Britain at the time, but progressive thinkers had started to see it as a solution to the problem of overfilled and insanitary cemeteries.

The practice of burning bodies is ancient, but in Western Europe, cremation was curtailed by the coming of Christianity. Not only does the Bible command that the dead be buried, but Christ's entombment was seen as essential to his resurrection. Clearly, cremation avoided the process of decomposition and ensured that in times of plague the body would not be a threat to the living. During battles, cremation ensured there was no desecration to the fallen soldiers or their graves, as the ashes could easily be taken away for proper rites and honour away from the enemy.

During the 19th century, cremation began to be considered as a suitable alternative. The poet Shelley's remains were burned on a beach in Italy, not terribly successfully, however, as his heart remained intact and was sent back to his wife. Experimental cremations took place in several people's back gardens in the 1870s, in the same decade as the issue was debated in the medical journal *The Lancet*, and the British Cremation Society was formed. Cremation was not new to the poor, of course. As a 19th-century gravedigger described one cemetery: "You should go there of a night, sometimes, Sir, and see them burning the bones and the coffins. You see, they dig up the 'commonses' every twelve years . . . and what they find left of them they burn."

The Cremation Society was formed by royal surgeon Sir Henry Thompson on January 13, 1874, and among the founders were Sir John Tenniel, immortalised as the illustrator of *Alice's Adventures in Wonderland*, the novelist Anthony Trollope, world-famous painter John Everett Millais and Sir T. Spencer-Wells. In 1879, they cremated a horse, but Home Secretary Sir Richard Cross threatened legal action if they cremated a dead human. Sir Henry wrote a paper entitled *The Treatment of the Body After Death*, published in *The Contemporary Review* for January, 1874. His main reason for supporting cremation was that "it was becoming a necessary sanitary precaution against the propagation of disease among a population daily growing larger in relation to the area it occupied".

Although the main argument he advanced was a sanitary one, other reasons are not lacking. Cremation, he believed, would prevent premature burial, would reduce the expense of funerals, would spare mourners the necessity of standing exposed to the weather during interment, and the ashes, kept in urns, would be safe from vandalism. Sir Henry Thompson boldly advanced a further economic, technical argument; namely, that the ashes might be used as fertilizer!

An able reply from Mr Holland, Medical Inspector of Burials for England and Wales, opposing the innovation as not being a sanitary necessity, elicited a second, more powerful, paper from Sir Henry Thompson. This provoked lively discussion and intense controversy in the press and Sir Henry, himself, received over 800 letters from the public. Eventually, they obtained ground at Woking to build the first crematorium, but were restricted from using it by the Home Office.

The inhabitants of Woking showed strong antipathy to the crematorium and, led by the vicar, a small but zealous deputation appealed to Sir Richard Cross to prohibit the use of the building. Despite also hearing the case of the Cremation Society, the Home Secretary, fearing cremation might be used to prevent the detection of death following violence or poison, refused to allow it until Parliament had authorised it by either a general or special act. With the threat of either legal or parliamentary proceedings against them, the Cremation Society was forced to abandon further experiments. From March, 1879, the function of the Society was restricted to trying to change the public attitude to cremation.

Cross Keys, Llantrisant where Dr Price met Gwenllian before cremating the infant.

Price planned to cremate his son on a hilltop of East Caerlan above Llantrisant, complete with Druidic lamentations on 13 January, 1884. Some reports claim he even told police and locals that he intended to burn the tiny corpse. The paraffin cask was ordered on Saturday, January 12, for the ceremony, from the wife of John MacCarthy, a hawker of Brynsadler. It was collected by Thomas Tootell, landlord of the Bute Arms, Pontyclun, who left with his horse and trap at six o'clock on Sunday evening, accompanied by Gwenllian Llewellyn.

Leaving her at Ty'r Clettwr, Tootell met the doctor at the Cross Keys Hotel on High Street, Llantrisant, and was soon rejoined by Gwenllian. That was where he gave his final instructions. He would climb the hill above, crossing two fields, and in the third field, owned by Price himself, would set down the cask and oil on the summit of Caerlan, a position that commanded views of the surrounding countryside and could be seen for miles, and cremate the child. At 7.15pm, as two local colliers, Uriah Wilkins and Lewis Ajax, were walking home from church on the wintry night, they saw the smoke rising from East Caerlan. They climbed the hill and walked through Price's fields to find the doctor engaged in the most macabre of events.

Dr Price, clad in a white robe, his hair and beard streaming in the wind, his arms outstretched as if on a crucifix, was chanting a lament in unintelligible Welsh. Before him was the cask of paraffin oil and within it a baby's corpse, carefully wrapped in napkins. Was this an action to protest about public hygiene and therefore a support of the work of the Cremation Society's aims to find an alternative method of disposal of the dead, or simply because he saw it as a Druidic rite lost with the growth of Christianity?

He called out a somewhat corrupted version of a poem written by the sixth century bard, Taliesin, which occurs in "Angar Cyvyndawd". It would seem to have been a lament on the soul's ascent to meet the Druidic bard:

> *"Pedair tywarchen*
> *Ni wys ei gorphen*
> *Pwy foch new Cwrwyden hudd*
> *Ath gyfarthaf, fawr Gadfardd?*
> *Gwr eith gynydd*
> *Ysgyrn niwl,*
> *Rhwyddynt ddau*
> *Rhaiadr gwynt;*
> *Traethallor yng ngolwg*
> *Yr efrau yn ngoddeg;*
> *Yr efrau yn efrog;*
> *Yr efrau yn efrau*
> *Bu Tes;*
> *hen anwylid, chywyd;*
> *Gwr a rod pan ei ddychwelyd;*
> *Cu welir crymdu, crymdwyn.*
> *Ladatum, laudate Deus."*

Until then, Llantrisant folk condoned Dr Price's actions as pure eccentricity, but this was just too much to comprehend. For the church and chapel-goers, it was the ultimate act of blasphemy. Thoughts of his well-known Druidic beliefs and their association of that cult with human sacrifice, swept away the affectionate good humour which had indulged his eccentricities. Although not understanding his ways, the villagers had felt that his reputation for miraculous cures and the mystery of his ceremonies had earned him their respect, although a respect mixed with fear. Now it was being outraged.

All the village knew that a child of about five months, blasphemously named Iesu Grist, had died in the doctor's house at 10 o'clock on Thursday night. The men who climbed the mountain to be faced with this macabre sight had many unanswered questions. Did the baby really die? Was this a human sacrifice? If not, then at best it was the desecration of the dead. At first, no one stirred as the flames leapt four or five feet into the darkness, and the doctor gazed into the heavens.

Villagers, returning from chapel, were transfixed at the sight of the burning pyre, although few realised the extent of the act being carried out in their own, close-knit community. Steadily, an unruly mob of locals multiplied on the mountain. Hearing of the disturbance, Police Sergeant William Hoyle of Llantrisant Police Station arrived, fearing the crowd was growing large. He kicked the barrel hard enough for it to fall and the burning corpse roll out. Although wrapped in napkins, its gruesome content was clear as the bare chest and exposed arms and legs were well alight. The mob broke into a frenzy, shrieking at the sight of the burning baby's corpse. Albert Davies, a local labourer, hooked a stick into the body and dragged it, still blazing, across the grass to the hedge, where he could get some turf to extinguish the burning flesh and napkins. Davies strenuously denied Price's later allegations that he had beaten and hooked the body about the head with his stick. Shock, horror, outrage and hatred swelled through the crowd, now numbering two or three hundred people, who became actively hostile and determined to push Price into the barrel amidst calls of "Let us burn the old devil."

The situation was saved by Police Constable Philip Francis (No. 163), a man noted for his way with rough public houses, who drew his truncheon and threatened to strike the first man who touched Price. The elderly doctor did not share this view of the part that Francis played as his protector, but said he thought he was being dragged off "like a felon" and was put in the cell at Llantrisant Police Station on George Street. The crowd themselves did not disperse with the removal of Price, but stayed on the fields and near the house until three o'clock in the morning, awaiting his return and, perhaps, the hope of more excitement.

Sergeant Hoyle travelled to Pontypridd to see his colleague Sergeant Evan Jones, who was unwilling to share in the responsibility of charging the Archdruid. They visited superintendent Jabez Matthews at 2am, who was sleeping soundly in his home at Berw Road and called from the bedroom window, telling them to keep Price locked up until morning, when the local magistrate would hear his case. He was made comfortable in the cell until 7am, with coats, two rugs, two blankets and a fire to keep him warm. Suspicions grew ever greater over Price's actions, questioning whether he had murdered the infant and was desperately trying to destroy all evidence. On the following morning, he was taken to Pontypridd by the direction of the Stipendiary Magistrate for the District, Mr Gwilym Williams (1839-1906), of Miskin Manor, a well-respected Freeman of the Town and later the grandfather of Sir Brandon Rhys Williams, Conservative MP for Kensington. The magistrate, whose statue stands in the vicinity of Cardiff law courts at Cathays Park, had been a stipendiary for Pontypridd and Rhondda since 1872, and well known as the "terror of malefactors." He bailed Dr Price to appear to the charge of misdemeanour in common law in not burying the body decently.

Sergeant Hoyle discussed the possibility of the child being murdered with Coroner E. B. Reece, supported by Superintendent Matthews. The infant had died suddenly and there were no birth or death certificates. The public wanted justice to be done, but the four believed in discussing it with Price without recourse to an inquest.

"There is no desire on the part of the coroner to hold an inquest if you will allow a medical man to see the child", was the letter delivered on the morning of January 15. Price, however, saw no reason why this should be necessary. He did not believe in registration and throughout the ensuing court hearings would not involve Gwenllian Llewellyn, refusing to admit she was even the mother of the baby.

An inquest was held on January 15, the same day as a small headline appeared in the *Western Mail* reading "Extraordinary scene on a Llantrisant mountain – Dr Price cremating a child". It took place at Llantrisant Police Station before the Coroner, and a jury, of which Mr Roderick Lewis, of the Wheatsheaf Hotel on High Street, was the foreman. A post mortem examination had been made by Dr Davies of Llantrisant, Dr Martin Davies of Bridgend and Dr William Davies. Gwenllian was sworn in but she objected to giving evidence as she understood that the object of the inquest was to commit her for a crime of which she knew nothing. The Coroner told her unless she gave evidence she would go to jail. She refused and was taken away by Superintendent Matthews. Dr Price was called and immediately suggested he ought not to be examined because there was a possibility of his being charged with killing the child. Price even refused to verify whether Iesu was Gwenllian's child, but admitted it was his own. Awkwardness prevailed throughout the entire hearing, until Price explained that the child fell ill the previous week. Teething pains took place and convulsions supervened. He was up two or three nights with the child and took extreme care and precaution, but on Thursday night he died in a convulsion.

Dr Price went on to explain that the child had not been christened but would have been, if it had lived, on the Rocking Stone, because that was where he had christened Hiarlles Morganwg decades before. They continued to argue over registering the child, with Price explaining, "But we Welsh bards, and I consider myself a Welsh bard, teach that it is not necessary to register or baptise, and that ultimately this will be the universal belief of the Island of Britain."

The Coroner replied, "But it is for the time being, you see, necessary."

Eventually, Gwenllian came before the Coroner again and gave the same explanation as Price over the health of the baby. Once the Coroner was satisfied, she was allowed to go. After hearing the evidence of Dr Naunton Wingfield Davies that the post mortem examination showed the child to be suffering from malnutrition for a long time prior to death, and that the death itself was due to asphyxia which might have been produced by convulsions, the jury returned a verdict of death from natural causes and not foul play.

The police made an application to the Coroner to bury the child, but Dr Price objected and demanded he had the body back, refusing to say whether he would attempt to burn it again. Superintendent Matthews intervened to suggest that perhaps the burial order should be handed over to him for transfer to Price if he promised, on his word of honour, to bury the child decently, or Matthews could keep the body until after the magisterial proceedings.

Price insisted on his rights, but Matthews won the day and the doctor left with the burial order and remarked threateningly, "You do as you like, and I shall do just as I like."

Dr Price was brought before the Stipendiary Magistrate, Mr Gwilym Williams, at Pontypridd on Wednesday, 16 January, 1884. Prosecutor Mr Rhys, of the firm of W. H. Morgan and Rhys, asked for a remand so the case could be thoroughly investigated. Price applied to the Stipendiary for instant delivery of the child then lying in Llantrisant Police Station. The judge felt Price's conduct with the baby was "an outrage" and had violated the residents of the town with his act. He was willing, if the doctor gave his word, to release the body as long as he disposed of it in the usual manner. Dr Price gave his word and the police were ordered to deliver the body in a box, covered in napkins.

Dr Price and his bail, Daniel Pritchard, were then bound over for £100 each, for the attendance of Price at the proceedings on the following Wednesday. Between six and seven o'clock that evening, Price, with his manservant Emmanuel John, better known as Y Mochyn Du (The Black Pig), went to the police station to collect the body. He took it to a building somewhere on Heol y Sarn, to feed a fat cow he kept there and, by the light of a candle, they chopped up three buckets of swedes.

As he had left the police station only hours before bearing the body of Iesu Grist, four men watched with curiosity as Price and his companion took the body in the building. They waited outside, but when the sound of chopping was heard, a menacing crowd gathered to listen to what they thought was the doctor dismembering the body. He innocently emerged to face a crowd so hostile he was forced to find a safe shelter from hurtling stones and sticks in The Bear Inn, instead of being able to go home with his manservant and the body. Eventually retreating to Ty'r Clettwr at 11pm, after climbing a series of garden walls, he hid the body under his bed until the time came for a second cremation.

The Bear Inn, Llantrisant

Earlier that night, the infuriated mob attacked his house while Gwenllian was alone inside. The incident began with one of the crowd hurling a stone through the window of Ty'r Clettwr. Fortunately for Gwenllian, the door was locked and she had four of the doctor's wolfish-looking dogs in the room, who barked furiously. She also reached for two of the pistols kept in the house and loaded them both, warning the mob not to try and enter.

At Pontypridd Police Court on the following Wednesday, Price appeared to answer the charge before Mr Ebenezer Lewis, Dr Leigh and Francis Crawshay. Superintendent Matthews asked for another week's adjournment, which was granted. On Wednesday, January 30, Dr Price appeared again before Mr Gwilym Williams, Dr Leigh, Francis Crawshay and Mr Rees. The whole story had started with the failure of Gwenllian, to register the birth of the child. She said Price was adverse to registration and she was fined £2.00 for it. Apparently she was summonsed by Judge Williams for assaulting P. C. Francis. The police officer said he met Gwenllian on the road to Llantrisant and tried to serve her with a notice that she had been fined for the non-registration of a child. She said: "I will have nothing to do with it." He tried to put it in her hand, and she struck him with her fist on his left ear. He again offered her the notice and she snatched a cane from her left hand and struck him with it across the right side of his face and ear. She later admitted the incident in the court, adding, "The police watch me like a cat watching a mouse and they threaten to take me to the police station as if I were a highway robber or a murderer. I told him I would not take it in the street."

The magistrate reminded her: "Because Dr Price is notorious, don't think that gives you any power outside the law. You must be dealt with like any ordinary person."

Mr Rhys then charged Price: "That he did, on the 13th of January, 1884, unlawfully, wilfully, and indecently attempt to cremate the body of his infant male child, and that he offered indignities to the remains of the said body; that by such conduct he caused a public nuisance; with attempting to dispose of the dead body of his male child, knowing that the coroner intended to hold an inquest on it, and without notice to the Coroner; that he did burn the said body, create such a stench as to be a public nuisance. With neglecting to give a Christian burial to the remains of the said body.

"I also charge Gwenllian Llewellyn with having committed the second and third offence and I shall call evidence that she went to the shop to fetch the oil and hired a conveyance to carry it to the place where the child was burnt, that she and the defendant were last seen together in the spot where the occurrence took place and within a few minutes of their being together, the cask of oil was set alight and illuminated the whole country around, and on this evidence I shall ask your worships to say she is equally guilty with Price of the attempt to cremate the child."

He went on to explain that cremation was only carried out scientifically and would fill others with feelings "of horror and disgust, as I think every right-minded person comparing our system of burial with that adopted by the defendant, must come to the conclusion that it is a far better way to carry the dead decently covered to a place of burial, followed by sympathetic friends and neighbours paying every token of respect to the memory of the dead one than to get hold of the nearest empty barrel, put a quantity of oil in it, and throw the dead body, partly exposed naked into it, and set fire to the whole lot . . . being accompanied by howling of a justly enraged public."

Rhys went on to call Price's actions "monstrous", and the idea of cremation as "new-fangled funeral pyre". It would appear in everyone's back garden, under the windows of their neighbours, leaving half-charred remains of dead bodies, he claimed.

"Until the Act of Parliament justifying cremation is passed, the common law must prevail and anyone acting in defiance of it must bear the pains and penalties of so acting," he added. Gwenllian was not present and it was resolved not to proceed with the charge against her on that occasion. Dr William Price pleaded not guilty.

At first, it seemed they would also proceed with matters arising out of the alleged child-chopping incident, but these were withdrawn through lack of evidence. The Stipendiary committed Price for trial at the Assizes on the two main charges. He was given bail in the sum of £100, with Mr Griffiths Evans of Pontypridd as his surety.

According to the *Western Mail* of that week, "The cockerels belonging to Dr Price, which went away when the doctor was taken to the police station, have now returned, none the worse for their travels. It is said that when the birds saw the doctor, they uttered a shrill chorus and seemed delighted to see him again."

He was committed for trial on Tuesday, 12 February, 1884, and the case of Regina v Price was opened at the Glamorganshire Winter Assizes in the Town Hall of Cardiff before Justice James Stephen. Price was one of 41 prisoners to appear before the court and one of "superior education" to the rest. Also in court was Henry Edward Coleman, aged 11, and friend William Rees, aged 10, charged with stealing a cake and five knives. Also, Mary Morris of Merthyr, charged with stealing a blanket.

In stark contrast, there was Dr Price himself, indicted for attempting to burn the body of his child instead of burying it. The second indictment was for trying to burn the body of a baby that had not been registered, to prevent an inquest being held upon it. A Grand Jury, including Mr S. Knight-Richards, the Lord Mayor of Cardiff, were sworn in. S. S. Hughes Q.C. and B. T. Williams appeared for the prosecution. Typically, Dr Price appeared undefended.

Justice Stephen told the court: "William Price is charged with a misdemeanour under the following circumstances: He had in his house a child five months old of which he is said to have been the father. The child died and Price, as it seems, did not register its death. The coroner accordingly gave him notice on Saturday, 12th January, 1884, that unless he sent a medical certificate of the cause of the child's death (the coroner) would hold an inquest on the body on the following Monday.

"Price on the Sunday afternoon took the body of the child to a field of his own, some distance from the town of Llantrisant, put it into a ten gallon cask of petroleum and set the petroleum on fire. A crowd collected, the body of the child burning was covered with earth, and the flames were extinguished, and Price was brought before the magistrates and committed for trial.

"He will be indicted before you on a charge which in different forms imputes to him as criminal in two parts of what he is said to have done. Namely, first, his having prevented the holding of an inquest on the body; and secondly, his having attempted to burn the child's body."

The judge pointed out that the coroner had no right to intrude on every death without adequate cause. He said nothing could justify the interference unless he was suspicious about the death if it had occurred by anything other than common illness. Justice Stephen went on to explain that he could not see why the coroner would find an inquest necessary in this particular case.

Secondly, the decision to cremate the body, which caused so much public attention, was not illegal. Justice Stephen explained "so far as I know, no legal decision upon it has ever been given."

After listing previous cases with regards to the disposal of the dead, Justice Stephen made this point: "After full consideration, I am of opinion that a person who burns instead of burying a dead body does not commit a criminal act, unless he does it in such a manner as to amount to a public nuisance at common law.

"My reason for this opinion is that upon the fullest examination of the authorities, I have been unable to discover any authority for the proposition that it is a misdemeanour to burn a dead body, and in the absence of such authority, I feel that I have no right to declare it to be one."

On Friday morning, February 15, at ten o'clock, before Mr Justice Stephen, Price appeared at the court with Hiarlles and an hour later was called by the clerk. He removed a blanket which concealed his singular costume of white smock of fine linen, with scalloped collar and cuffs, and a shawl of royal tartan over his broad shoulders, making a striking figure with his forceful eloquence.

His fine features, picturesque attire and long, white hair all added to the effect of the showman who had played so brilliantly to the court throughout the trial. During the hearings, he received thousands of letters from supporters, noting with satisfaction the way the world's press took down his words.

The twelve jurymen were called and the prosecution gave a brief outline of his work as a surgeon and his affinity with Druidic beliefs. He then proceeded to describe the cremation on East Caerlan. Prosecutors Hughes and Williams tried to persuade Justice Stephen that the cremation was a misdemeanour at common law, but he would not accept it. Price, the practised orator, gave an admirable performance in the court, outlining how disgusting the decomposition of a body in a coffin could be. He explained that if properly done and out of the sight of others, then cremation was the most acceptable form of disposing of a body.

Price proclaimed: "It is not right that a carcass should be allowed to rot and decompose in this way. It results in a wastage of good land, pollution of the earth, water and air, and is a constant danger to all living creatures."

He received support from the hygienist Sir John Simon (1816-1904). Price also launched an unprecedented attack on Albert Davies, the one who dragged the corpse "64 yards" from the flames, claiming his actions were far worse than the cremation itself. Again, Justice Stephen reiterated that the jury had to agree that there, indeed, was a criminal act to answer for. The jury were unable to agree on whether he had committed a crime or not, and after three hours of deliberation, the judge had them all dismissed and a new jury was found for a new trial on the following day.

A second jury met after lunch to discuss whether the disposal of the body without a death certificate and the opportunity for an inquest was a criminal act. Sergeant Hoyle was called to give evidence and said he warned Price beforehand not to cremate the child. Price had commented, "What has it to do with you or the coroner how I dispose of my child?"

Price explained to the court, "I was determined, before hearing from the coroner, to cremate the infant, and no one should have interfered with me to prevent me cremating it. If it had not been for the police offering to step in - they committed upon my property, my infant and myself, the most outrageous ill.

"I have no doubt that if the Llantrisant people had been left alone, they never would have interfered with me.

"But in consequence of the police being put on by the master hounds, by the bloodhounds that came upon me, the people followed them if you please. The people followed the police and took me as I had been a felon or a murderer, and took me from doing what has been practically done before.

"I consider it a better mode of dealing with all persons than poisoning the earth, poisoning the water, and poisoning the atmosphere. I have never shrunk from the idea, and if I cannot get somebody to burn me, I would burn myself if I could."

The judge turned to the jury and asked whether they thought Price's conduct gave the coroner reasonable ground to suppose that the child had died otherwise than from natural causes. They felt he was not guilty and were discharged. Price smiled, was congratulated by his colleagues, and left the court. On the following morning, the original charge was brought against him once more. But it was withdrawn with immediate effect. The prosecution decided that in the light of the previous day's events, they would not continue with the proceedings. Hughes added, "After the decision of your lordship that cremation is not illegal, I can only now hope that if it is practised at some subsequent occasion it will be done under less painful circumstances." On returning to Llantrisant, Dr Price and his daughter were met by a large crowd and the celebrations continued with the hanging of a flag on his home.

The *British Medical Journal* again hailed Price for his court case, "The recent case of Dr Price has awakened public interest once more to the consideration of a practice that is in every way to be commended, even from sentimental points of view, for there can be but one opinion as to the hygienic value of cremation; and clean ashes are surely less repulsive to contemplate than mouldering carcases.

"As Darwin has shown, the worms swallow earthy matter, and after separating the digestible portion they eject the remainder in little coils at the mouth of their burrows. In dry weather, the worm descends to a considerable depth, and brings up to the surface the particles which it ejects. Hence, earth infected by contiguity to a diseased carcass, buried with the greatest care, is brought to the surface and can infect a whole pasture."

Price celebrated his victory by bringing an action against the police who acted at the cremation of Iesu Grist. He instituted legal proceedings against Police Superintendent Matthews of Pontypridd and Sergeant Hoyle of Llantrisant for false imprisonment following the cremation, also malicious persecution by the detention of the body and defamation of his character. Price went to Swansea Assizes before Justice Grove in August and although action against Matthews was non-suited, the doctor recovered damages from Hoyle.

He successfully carried out his intention to cremate Iesu Grist on Friday, 14 March, 1884, unmolested by the crowds, although Pc Hoyle and Rowe were said to have watched the incident from the ruins of Llantrisant Castle. Most of the crowds stood at the foot of the hill and watched. Only Wheatsheaf Inn landlord Roderick Lewis dared go closer to confirm the event took place. Locals thought the body had been buried, others wondered whether the remains were burnt in a large oven at Ty'r Clettwr. In fact, the body was eventually burned in half a ton of coal, a gallon of paraffin oil and sixpenny worth of wood. The entire act cost 8s 2d. A pair of iron grids were placed above the coal and the box containing the child, wrapped in napkins, above. Again, Price chanted an ancient song in the presence of a number of unorthodox spectators, most notably some 20 horned cattle, driven to the site by the doctor and his servant, Mochyn Du. The ashes were carried away in the winds.

Dr Price decided to commemorate the cremation by having an oval-shaped medal struck in bronze, and over 3,000 of these were sold at 3d each. He once explained, "The Serpent represents the Cymmerian race and the Cymmerian language, and the only word that is enunciated by the serpents' "sth" - a hissing sound which is represented by the vowels which surround it.

"Now in the goat, the serpent, and the letters of his egg, or oval over his head, I am able to decipher the pedigree of the poet, and it is so follows:

The bronze coin to commemorate Iesu Grist's cremation.

"I will go to sow him who will sow me who will go to sow him. They will sow perpetual motion in the Serpent of Baptism with the Light of the Brain of the Cymmerian goat.

"The goat is the scapegoat of the wilderness, which governed the world for all eternity and the serpent circumscribes the world. The verse you see on the obverse side of the medal was composed by me, and a free translation of it would run thus:

The Welsh words on the rear of the commemorative coin

"See Jesus Christ from the fire dragging

In the hand of Victoria, my dear Welshman,

In the presence of the Day of Judgement he owns the sword

Of the Prince of Love, and the Crown of Wales.

January 13 1884."

The actual words on the coin written in Welsh are:

"Gwel Jessu Crist o yr tan yn llysgo
Yn llaw Victoria, ym annwyl Gymmro
Ang gwydd y varn ve bia cleddu
Tywysog Cariad Corron Cymmru
Ionawr yr 13 eg 1884"

The eccentric was not about to let matters lie, and just to create further stir in the town would often cremate his dead cattle on the mountainside. The cremation of Morgan the Bull was well documented at the time when he had the carcass carried to East Caerlan for a ritualistic disposal!

He next conceived the idea of building a public crematorium in the vicinity of Llantrisant, and made a public appeal for subscriptions. Letters of support were received from London, Europe and even India, but the project was discontinued. The court case was also celebrated in popular ballads which were sold in the fairs and markets of South Wales at the time. Welsh and English versions were usually printed on the same leaflet. Although their authors remain anonymous, they still make interesting reading.

"Our Bible tells us clearly
In words distinct and clear,
Our dust with dust shall mingle
Till Gabriel shall appear;
No word is ever written
About cremation dire,
The Bible does not mention
Of paraffin and fire!

"No doubt you're all acquainted,
And often have heard tell,
Of Doctor Price, Llantrisant,
And know his actions well;
He sought to put his infant
Amidst the raging flame,
But policemen came there quickly,
And stopped his little game.

"For that, at the Assizes
At Cardiff, he was tried,
But somehow or another
The Judge did with him side;
And thus said Justice Stephen
"A body you may now
Cremate as you think proper –
But don't kick up a row"

"It seems that any person
Can burn a corpse who please,
But grant that all good people
May keep from such affairs;
And may we all be buried
In tombs, peaceful and low,
To sleep until awakened
When loud the trump shall blow."

Later in 1884, an article relating to the cremation appeared in *Cassell's Saturday Journal* (For the Home of the People), a London newspaper. The article, called The Blood Stone Tragedy, recalls the story of Price and Iesu Grist. What is all the more significant about the 3,000 line article is that it was written by a 25-year-old Scottish writer named Arthur Conan Doyle. The writer had obviously followed Price's escapades as they had appeared in the national press. Also a bachelor of medicine and master of surgery, Doyle was a budding author, living in Portsmouth by 1883 and a prolific member of a local literary circle. Four years later and the writer published *A Study in Scarlet*, introducing a new detective to the literary world, named Sherlock Holmes.

Gwenllian remained with Dr Price for the rest of his long life and bore him two further children. On 8 October, 1884, Iesu Grist II was born, and Price believed he would inherit all his Druidic wisdom. Only after the doctor's passing was the child renamed Nicholas, possibly in memory of his great-great grandfather, the Pentyrch ironmaster, or possibly to Dr Price's brother who died as a child. On 27 May, 1886, Gwenllian gave birth to a daughter called Penelopen Elizabeth.

Iesu Grist II was born in 1884.

Undoubtedly, the doctor fathered numerous children throughout the districts in which he lived. As he championed the cause of the unmarried mother at the height of Queen Victoria's long reign, it naturally made him even more unpopular. He wrote:

"Marriage is of no importance, rather is it the desire to mate which Nature has endowed in us which makes people complete the union which we call marriage. I have found it unnecessary to enter into legal marriage, because I do not, as an evolved being, require any law or religious ceremony to compel me to love the woman I have chosen as my mate.

"The artificial thunder of the church and the state on marriage cannot frighten me to live with a woman under compulsion. No law made by God or man can compel a man and a woman to love each other, but it can and does compel them to live with each other, which is quite another thing."

Chapter Nine

The Eccentric

WITH age, Dr Price's general conduct became increasingly bizarre, adding to the ever-growing array of stories about him. Undoubtedly, he was a gifted surgeon and his services were in great request in complicated cases or when other practitioners pronounced a hopeless situation. His mode of treatment was extraordinary, but the public's total faith in his skill was unbounded and people went long distances to consult him in his basic home of bare walls and a consulting room, which testified to his disregard for bodily comforts. He was even sent for, to travel to patients at great expense, as a last resort.

As Dr Cule explained, "Dr Price had what counsel in "Fothergill and Price" described as "lucid intervals". Indeed, he never broke down to the gross degree to which his father deteriorated. The eccentricities and oddities, the zeal and aggression of his youth became more florid with age, but he retained sufficient integration to be a formidable opponent, even in old age. He is remembered in Wales for his eccentricities, his dress, his mystical Druidism and ceremonial. The newspapers of his time showed him as a comic-tragic figure playing a clownish part on the stage. The mumbling shambles of his appearance at Blaenau as an old man who undressed to the audience should not be recalled without remembering Lady Charlotte Guest's description of his eloquence. His clashes with the "regular Druids" must recall his efforts to provide an earlier Welsh Folk Museum!"

People derided his flamboyance, but no one could mock at his fame as a successful physician and surgeon, just as the ill-paid miners could not complain of his habit of giving them his services free of charge. He also was known to assist, professionally, materially and spiritually, outcast girls condemned by the chapel.

A documented tale was that of a young girl in Llantrisant, dying of a stomach complaint. Dr Price ordered the parents to fill a clay pipe with tobacco and make her swallow the smoke. They didn't carry out the orders and she died.

When he held an autopsy, he opened her stomach and found a live snail. On blowing pipe smoke fumes at the creature, it died. However, the fact the Price was totally against smoking, somehow refutes these claims.

Once, when he went to see a dying woman in a remote village, a man who suffered from rheumatism consulted him.

"How long have you used these crutches?" asked Dr Price.

"For two years, sir," was the reply.

A drawing of Dr Price dressed in one of his military uniforms.

Dr Price said, "Put the crutches away. You need the medicine of movement. If you refuse to use your limbs, they become useless. I will now take away your stick, walk again, as you first did as a child and then learn to walk like a man." After this elementary physiotherapy, with a little embrocation, his movement was restored.

An old Welsh woman once asked the doctor for "something for the headache." Dr Price asked to be allowed to look into her bonnet.

The woman, surprised, handed him her head-gear, which was thickly lined with two layers of flannel, irrespective of the straw and trimmings, whereupon the doctor examined it, and said, "No wonder you have a headache. This thatch is fourteen ounces too heavy. Reduce the weight, and the headache will go."

Another piece of common sense diagnoses and treatments was down to a patient suffering from over-indulgence in food and drink. He was told that the trouble was due to "consumption - table consumption of the most hopeless kind. No cure unless you live lower and eat less."

Price was called to the Pontypridd farm of Evan Evans and was not surprised to find him groaning in pain and clutching his stomach. The old farmer, a widower with two sons and a daughter, was renowned for his heavy drinking.

Leaving the farmer in agony on his bed, Price went downstairs to meet Evan's 21-year-old daughter, Megan, and together they walked to a nearby pond, where Price caught a frog. Returning to the farmhouse, he instructed Evan to take some medicine which made him vomit in a bucket in which the doctor placed the frog.

Appearing shocked, Price convinced Evans that beer was causing the growth of frogs in his stomach and the farmer was so appalled, he never drank again. He paid Price a £2.00 fee, which the doctor secretly returned to the family. Historians have since argued that Megan was Dr Price's first partner, and the mother of Hiarlles. Others confirm it was, indeed, Ann Morgan of Pentyrch.

Another farmer once asked him, "What shall I do, Dr Price? I'm as stiff as an old horse."

"Wash and be clean," was the laconic reply. "With the dirt of half a century upon your body, how can you expect to be anything but stiff?"

Price, apparently, had an interesting treatment for a dislocated shoulder. The story runs that it was his custom to walk from Llantrisant to Ystrad Mynach, where he would take the train to Rhymney.

One day, whilst on his walk in his usual garb, he noticed a group of people standing outside the door of a house in great distress. He enquired the nature of the trouble and was told a man had just been brought in with a dislocated shoulder. He went inside, placed a stool on which he told the man to stand and strongly grip a meat-hook that was protruding from the ceiling. The doctor kicked away the stool. The man fell, his shoulder jerked into place and the doctor continued on his journey.

One day, an old Rhondda man and his son called on Price and asked to give his opinion on his wife. Together, they walked to Penrhiwfer, a journey of several miles. After examining the patient, Price recommended a prescription that could only be made up by a chemist in Pontypridd, but despite the skill of the pharmacist, the woman died.

The relatives applied to Price for a death certificate. He gave it, believing that malnutrition was the blame and wrote, "Died through the laws of the land", on the certificate. They had to reply to another doctor for a proper certificate.

Dr Price's cure for rheumatism was said to be ginger and salts. "The ginger will penetrate where the salts will not, and the salts will work from there."

He would never eat rhubarb, simply because he noticed that animals never ate it either.

A lady was suffering from intractable pruritus, a skin complaint, for which there was no cause nor cure. Price invited her into his house and placed her in a room with a chair and table and commanded her to undress. Then, he gave her a kitten to hold under her armpit. In an hour, he returned to find her shivering with cold, but still holding the kitten.

The doctor took the animal away and demonstrated a large lump on her skin. He incised it and it released a mass of lice. Needless to say, she was cured.

A pretty girl was pining away, and her debilitated condition caused her mother such great anxiety that she took her to be seen by Dr. Price.

"Well, sir," said the mother, "what do you think is the matter with her?"

"Heart complaint," was the reply.

"I did think so," said the astute mother. "She do look that uncommon pale sometimes, and her breath is short and there's always them stitches in her side. Will you please, sir, to have the kindness to give her something for it?"

"I can do nothing for her - nothing whatever," said the doctor, who, observing the mother's anxious look, added, "Many waters cannot quench love, neither can floods drown it."

He once recommended the following treatment to a patient of his in Hopkinstown who was suffering from stomach and chest pain. The man was to fast for twenty-four hours, and on Saturday, his wife was to prepare the Sunday joint so it would be ready at noon, when the doctor would call. He arrived, and taking the joint from the oven, placed it on the man's bare chest. With carving knife in hand, he threatened the man that if he moved so much as an inch to taste a morsel of the joint, he could cut his throat.

They waited expectantly, and from the man's inside crawled up a worm that was so hungry it was attracted by the aroma! Once he killed the worm, the man was cured of his symptoms.

Although many of these events are recognisable as tall tales, they show the type of impression he made on his contemporaries. There is also a saga of anecdotes, which by their similarity also indicate the nature of the man.

There was the well-known tale of the local butcher who called on him to lay a complaint to a problem.

He asked the doctor, "If a dog entered some premises and stole a leg of lamb, what would you advise?

"Well, I would make the owner of the dog pay for the meat," the doctor said.

"Well, it was your dog sir."

"How much was the meat?" asked Price

"Five shillings," the butcher explained.

"Well, here is your money".

The delighted butcher was leaving when the doctor called him back. "You owe me six shillings and eight-pence".

"What for?"

"Legal advice", said the doctor.

One day, he admired a chest of drawers in a shop. The shopkeeper could see he liked it and said he would "send it down" to his home.

"As you like," replied the doctor.

Some time later, the keeper asked for payment and the doctor looked surprised. "Sold? You asked me if I liked it. I said I did. You said you'd send it down. It was a gift."

Price also recounted the story of a Will, when Thomas Thomas of Wern, near Nelson, called on him the night before he died. He explained he had not written a Will and when Price called for the attorney, who arrived just before midnight, the legal man refused to draw the paperwork that night. Instead, Price wrote his Will and the old man died before six o'clock the following morning. The Will was disputed because a claim was made that it was not finished before Thomas had signed it. In effect, the claim was Price had listened to Thomas's wishes, convinced him to sign the document and then filled in the necessary items after the death. But to prove there was legally "still life in the body" at the time of finishing the document, Price allegedly caught a fly and placed it in the deceased's mouth. The widow, in whose favour the Will was made, eventually proved successful.

Dr Price's friends were as peculiar as himself, particularly when remembering the picture of him sitting next to a man wearing a Wild West costume. Known as Dr Robert Richards Anderson of Fernhill, near Carmarthen, he was not a doctor and his name was actually Robert Ricketts Evans, and a note of the name change appeared in *The Times* in 1871. It is believed he assisted in the public execution of schoolteacher Charlie Peace (1832-1879), the notorious burglar and murderer of a policeman, Pc Cox, in Seymour Grove, Old Trafford.

Anderson's claims appear valid, given his nickname of Evans y Crogwr – Evans the Hangman, and his peculiar character made him something of a kindred spirit to Price. He died on 26 August, 1901, only a few years after lighting Dr Price's own cremation pyre.

Other friends included Dr Charles Fox, of the Quaker family. He was much younger than Price and after studying at The London Hospital, qualified with M.R.C.S. in 1873. and was placed on the Register in late 1874.

Dr Price with Dr Robert Richards Anderson.

He was one of the seven sons of Joseph John Fox (1821-1897), and shared many of Dr Price's views, particularly on vegetarianism and vaccination. He was a well-published medic and lived in a tent in the West Country for many years because he loved nature to such a degree. In later years, Dr Price led meetings in opposition to the "regular Druids" of Myfyr Morganwg on the rocking stone and it was obvious there was conflict between them on how superior one was to the other. Price considered himself a member of a hierarchical Druidic society than them. In interview shortly after Myfyr's death in 1888, he said: "He was a very clever old man and very well read, but he did not understand."

Dr William Price and friends

As for another of the tribe, the *Western Mail* journalist, Morien, who claimed to be Myfyr's successor, Price added "Well, Morien knows nothing of Druidism, not he. An Archdruid should be able to read and decipher all Druidical letters and hieroglyphics and Morien knows nothing at all about them."

Rhondda-born Owen Morgan, better known as Morien (1836-1921), was fascinated by local folklore, the details of which he gathered and studied, comparing them to similar traditions from around the world. He wrote from around 1870 until his death in 1921 about the local traditions of Druidism, the remnants of which he found in the oral traditions of the valleys of South Wales.

Under the influence of the fictions of Iolo Morganwg and Myfyr Morganwg, Morien wrote a number of books, which include *Pabell Dafydd* (1889), about the Druids, "*Kimmerian Discoveries*", on the alleged Chaldean origins of the Welsh, "*A Guide to the Gorsedd*" and "*A History of Pontypridd and the Rhondda Valleys*" (1903).

Owen Morgan (Morien)

Dr William Price & family

The last named, was described by R. T. Jenkins as "an odd jumble of Druidism, mythology, topography, local history and biography". Basically, this is one of the most unreliable local history books of the time.

From 1870 to 1899, Morien, who had settled in Glyntaf at a house known as Ashgrove, specialised in the reporting of mining disasters, of which there were many and to which his florid style was well-suited. As Professor Meic Stephens later claimed, "As a historian, Morien's grasp of his subject left a great deal to be desired.

What did it for Morien as a historian was Druidism, or more precisely Neo-Druidism, that feverish belief in the arcane and downright bogus, which had been propagated by the wayward genius of Iolo Morganwg."

Dr Price would also hold lectures, such as one on the Ancient Britons in Blaenau. He was welcomed by the Blaenau Brass Band, but the hall was only half full on a stormy night. Instead, he lectured on the death of Iesu and the cremation, and ignored the Britons. Then he stripped, causing women to run out of the hall as he took off his trousers, only to reveal the well-documented, skin-tight red outfit, covered in green letters from the bardic alphabet. In his left hand he held a pole, with horns, and a red streamer hanging down. The horns represented the crescent moon. He sang a Welsh song about his dress and then, to the amazement of the audience, donned his trousers.

He repeated the performance at the Cardiff Art Exhibition in April 1884. It was dramatically described in the *Cardiff Times* of April 12, "In a manner which had about it a touch of the occult, the lecturer connected his early ancestry with the contents of the Goose's Egg, and declared, amid wondering amusement on the part of the hearers, that 3,700 years ago his birth was registered, and thus, he said, he objected to registration now, this remark apparently having reference to the proceedings recent taken with view to the registration of the child Price cremated. The doctor struck up a Welsh song". He went on to undress, kick off his boots as the ladies left the room, only to be found wearing the costume covered in Druidic letters.

Chapter Ten

THE PASSING

A YEAR before his death, Dr William Price was injured after a fall from his carriage, when his horse slipped on an icy road near Llantrisant. For weeks he lay on the couch in the front room of Ty'r Clettwr, and eventually recovered, but had lost his zeal and energy. However, it was remarkable how youthful he continued to look, with several articles written at the time commenting on his clear and fresh-faced complexion. Only a few years earlier, he held an interview with the *South Wales Daily News*, the contents of which make remarkable reading. Sadly, since the doctor was 88 years old at the time, one can only imagine how mentally stable he actually was. Having said that, a significant amount of the interview appears to be true.

In his typical aggressive tone, he was quick to point out to the journalist on hand, Ap Idanfryn, that death was nothing at all. "Death! There is no death man!", he proclaimed. "That which you call death does not exist except in the imagination." When questioned why he often stated he would live to 120, he snapped: "People do not understand me when I speak. They cannot comprehend. They are ignorant. Do they think that I, who have existed upon this earth for ten thousand years, cannot tell what the future has in store for me?

"Death, indeed – I shall never die." Pointing to his second son, he said, "That child is my son – Iesu Grist. I shall, in future, exist in him. He is my offspring, and what takes place at what you call death is simply a renewal, when I shall exchange this body for that of my offspring."

After a series of treatments from Dr William Naunton Davies, who lived directly opposite him on High Street, Price recovered sufficiently from his fall to travel to Pontypridd, Cardiff and even Carmarthen that summer. He was not quite so buoyant as before, as his small stature began to stoop, but more visitors than ever came to Llantrisant to see him.

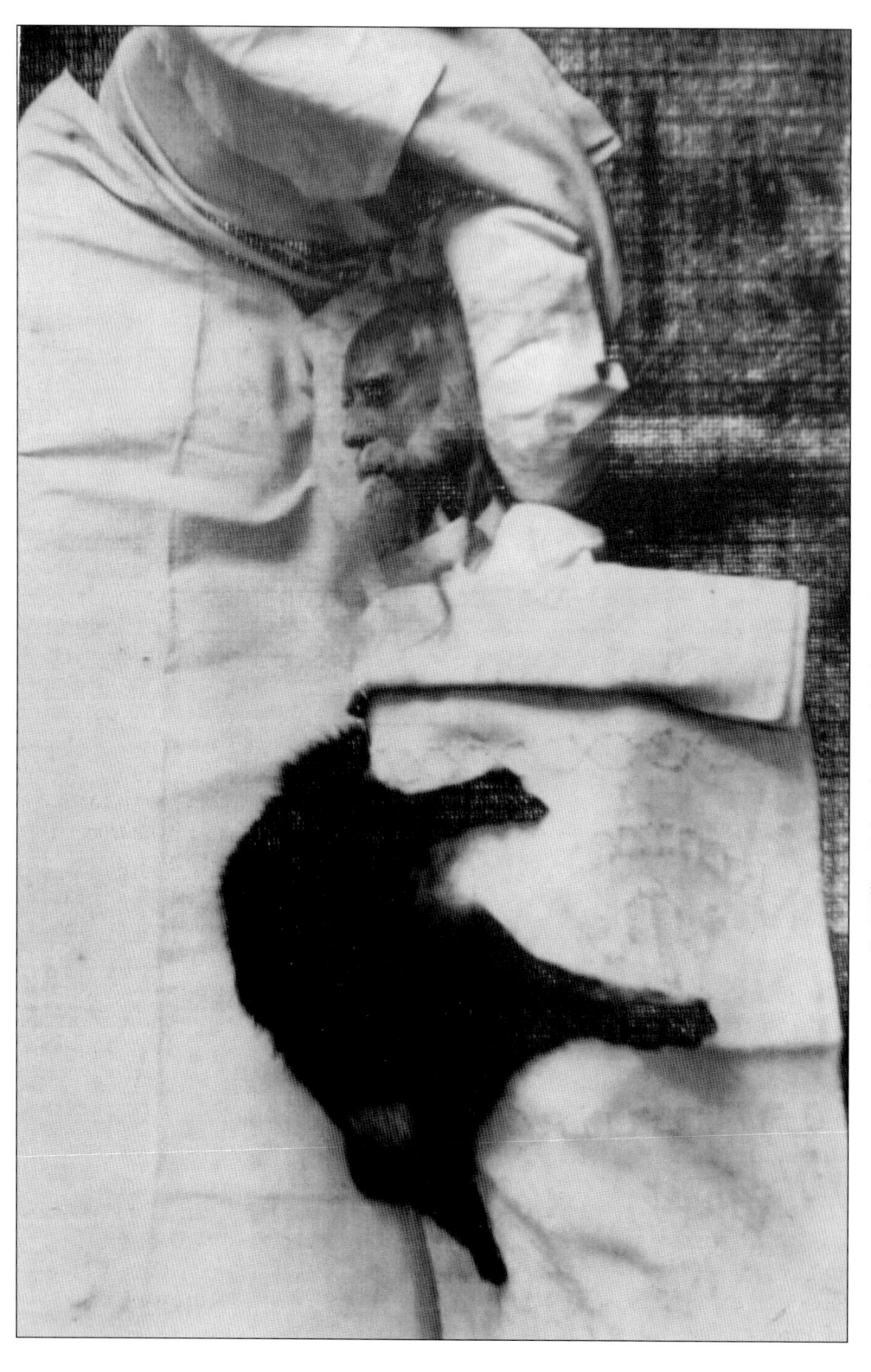

Dr William Price, photographed shortly after his death in 1893.

Going about his business, he still attended scores of afflicted patients who flocked to him from all parts of Wales, but gradually the grand old doctor became weaker.

He was already preparing for his cremation, having ordered a 61ft high, white pole to be placed on Caerlan fields where the event would take place. It was surmounted by a representation of the New Moon and could be seen for miles around. Some thought it was there to mark the spot where he cremated Iesu Grist, but the doctor wanted it to indicate the spot where his own body would be disposed of.

On 18 January, 1893, he stood on the front doorstep of Ty'r Clettwr, took a deep breath of air, and looked at the beautiful country landscape before him.

The 61ft high pole at Caerlan Fields to mark the spot of the cremation

During the previous year, he had not slept on his bed but on his couch, because of an aversion to feather beds. He came inside the house, lay on his couch and claimed, "Well, you have laid me on my couch at last. It is unlikely that I shall ever rise again". He added that he wouldn't die that night, or that week, but would not survive the fortnight. Sometimes he sat up, although he seldom spoke, but retained all his faculties. His eldest daughter, Hiarlles, travelled from Cardiff to help nurse him during his final days. Neighbour Mrs Sparnon also spent time in the house to help care for the ailing doctor. One morning, a letter from a friend was received and the doctor whispered, "then it must be answered", before fainting. Then, at 9pm on Monday, 23 January 1893, Gwenllian knelt by his side and asked him whether he would take some cider.

"No, give me champagne," he answered. After sipping from his glass, Dr William Price lay back and died peacefully and quietly. Gwenllian said, "It was as if a candle had gone out. There were no indications of pain and he seemed to have been sleeping tranquilly earlier in the day and he retained consciousness until the last minute."

Dr Naunton Davies said he scarcely considered the old doctor had been ill during the past year, as he had recovered from his fall and was wonderfully "hearty" for his age until his last illness overtook him. "He had retained his faculties to a wonderful degree until the last and the cause of death was senile decay - in fact, general failure." News of his death shocked the district, for although people realised his advanced age, it was still unexpected, since news of his illness was kept within the family.

Iesu Grist II (Nicholas) and Penelopen, pictured outside Ty'r Clettwr, in 1893.

Dr Price had no fear of death and felt it was a natural, physiological event that did not deserve sorrow or mourning. He gave explicit instructions on the disposal of his body in his Will, demanding it be cremated ("thus helping the grass to grow and the flowers to bloom"). Time and again, he'd told Gwenllian "Peidiwch a'm rhoi i yn y ddaear" (Do not put me in the ground) and he would add "Keep me on the surface of the earth."

When asked why she would not allow his body to be cremated at Woking Crematorium, she added, "The doctor had no faith in crematoriums of that kind. He desired that his body should be burned in the open air, and it shall be, if I get my way. My neighbours seem to think that it is not right he should be cremated. Their belief is in burials, but I should never forgive myself if I were to bury him. If I had the courage to see my own child cremated then surely I ought not to be afraid to cremate him."

She emphasised that no strangers should be allowed to revel in gazing on his dead body and it should be burned in a core of timber with two tons of coal and no attempt should be made at preserving his body. Gwenllian and her two children were appointed executors of the Will. Along with Hiarlles and Roderick Lewis, they took the police in their confidence and discussed plans for a cremation with Mr E. John J.P., the local magistrate. Together, they resolved to carry out the cremation ceremony with decency and free from molestation.

Price had written in his Will that he should be placed in the chair of his uncle Hugh Jones of Gelliwastad, Machen "and deposit it on one cord of wood and two tons of coal piled up within the triangle on Caerlan with the face of the pile saturated with paraffin then fire the pile where it shall be burned every atom . . . the dust retaining only in the triangle shall be sown to grow grass and natural flowers."

It was the first pre-arranged cremation in Wales and hundreds of admission tickets were issued for the major event. No matter how much they tried, many people failed to gain entry. Even a member of the Royal College of Surgeons tried to get four tickets, but failed. The police and printers were inundated with demands but were not allowed to distribute them. The tickets, printed by Davies Bros of the *Chronicle Office*, Pontypridd, read: "Tuesday, Jan 31 '93: Cremation of Dr Price. Admit bearer. Gwenllian Llewellyn."

As the day approached, the applications and letters of sympathy grew. One came from a "Fellow Practitioner" in Aberdare, seeking tickets for himself, while a Llandaff resident and one time patient of the doctor, wrote to Miss Llewellyn, "Kindly allow me to express my deep sympathy with you and the little ones in your bereavement.

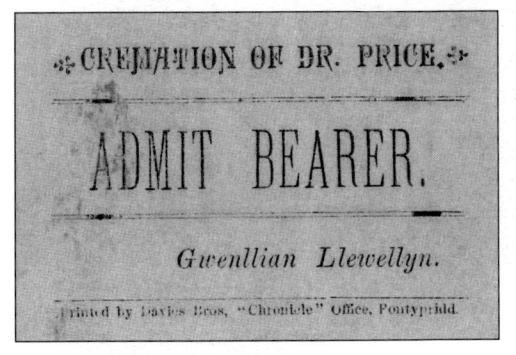

The admission ticket to the cremation.

"Ever since my first acquaintance with Dr Price, I have always admired him for his manliness and his skill as a practitioner. I should be very pleased to pay what respect I can, and if you have any tickets to spare me I would feel greatly obliged, as the only way in which I can testify my respect is by attending the ceremony of cremation.

"I know from the daily papers you are greatly pressed with correspondence, therefore I will not trouble you further, but on behalf of the children accept my sincere sympathy."

Another letter from William Evans of the Wimborne Hotel, Cardiff, read, "Sorry for your bereavement, as I have been a great friend of the deceased gentleman in his great trials through this carnal world. I beg on you to send me a few tickets to see him cremated."

Another, from Robert Williams of Bank Chambers, Pontypool, and dated January 25, read, "When I inquired of you on Monday morning last how the aged Dr Price was, I did not expect to hear so soon of his death. Pray accept my sympathies both for yourself and children in the loss you have sustained.

Residents besieged Ty'r Clettwr for admission tickets.

"Understanding by this morning's paper that the doctor will be cremated, and being a member of the Cremation Society of England, and also an occasional lecturer in favour of cremation, I would esteem it a great favour to be allowed to witness the cremation of the body of one who, without doubt, settled the legal difficulties as to cremation in this country."

One of Morien's reports also claims that a Mr J. Loveless, architectural stone and wood carver, of Severn Road, Canton, Cardiff, had visited Ty'r Clettwr and took a plaster cast of the head and face of the doctor. At first, it was agreed that the cremation would take place at midday, but rumours grew that the family were, in fact, preparing to start the proceedings much earlier.

The house on Cremation day

As word spread of the change in plan, people began arriving at Llantrisant by 4am, coming by brakes, horses, or on foot, and by the time the funeral procession began, there was an estimated 20,000 headed for East Caerlan. Every road was congested as the carnival mood prevailed, much to the doctor's wishes, and the pubs ran dry of ale. Ty'r Clettwr was besieged with visitors requesting tickets.

One poet even sold copies of his work *The Life and Death of Dr Price*, littering it with errors - particularly where it read that he had cremated a daughter and not a son! Dr Price had already designed his coffin, which was constructed by Thomas Jones, a blacksmith, of Talbot Green. The casket was made of sheet iron, encircled with iron bands and draped with white muslin. Jones felt iron would be red-hot in the flames but would not crack, so there was no chance of the body becoming exposed. A series of holes along the side were placed to allow the flames to enter and for fumes to disperse.

The scene outside Ty'r Clettwr as admission tickets were handed out.

109

LINES ON THE DEATH AND CREMATION OF

The Grand Old Welshman

ARCH-DRUID DOCTOR PRICE

WHO DIED AT LLANTRISSANT, MONDAY, JAN. 23rd, 1893

IN HIS 93rd YEAR,

AND HIS REMAINS CREMATED SHORTLY AFTER HIS DEATH.

"LOG CABIN"

A grand old Cambrian Chieftain has just passed away,
  From the land that we know he loved so well,
Doctor Price the Druid you have known for many a day
  And Llantrissant his history can tell.
Descended he could show, from centuries ago,
  He has left the dear old mountains now at last ;
And nearly ninety-three we're told that he must be,
  A missing link between this and the past.

Llantrissant knew him well, he wants no funeral knell
  No hypocrites in mourning him bewails,
If they carried out his wishes, they have done right well
  For Doctor Price the grand Arch-Druid of South Wales

His Ancestors they were Druids when Llewellyn reigned as
  When the ancient Minstrels sang among the hills, [king
The Retainers in our Castles made the valleys ring,
  And love of Country every bosom fills.
Not one shadow of disgrace in our history can we trace,
  Our enemies try to do it but they fail ;
And now the old man's departed we shall miss the face
  Of Doctor Price the grand Arch-Druid of South Wales

If you saw him in the market his dress may have been queer
  But he could please himself what he should wear,
His rough and ready costume was respected here,
  To insult him I'm sure there's no one dare.
In Cremation he believed, and so he had conceived,
  His principles of Religion he would show ;
To burn the useless body if the Soul's in heaven received
  As the Druids did a thousand years ago.

Once had a daughter who died some years ago,
  At his farm 'neath the shadow of the hill,
Her body was Cremated as in Pontypridd they know,
  And 'twas said he had committed a sin until—
The Magistrates found he could stand his ground,
  And no one now that incident bewails ;
For many English people as the years pass around,
  Have left a will the same as Doctor Price of Wales.

In his will he plainly stated what he wanted them to do
  To take his body as he died into the fields ;
The old ancient City of Caerleon close in view,
  The pure air of Heaven above him to be revealed,
He said take me away at the middle of the day
  Let my ashes scatter as the breezes blow,
And where I was Cremated at some future day
  Let the grass and the lovely flowers grow.

The fine old race of Welshmen are leaving us so fast,
  There are few that now are left behind ;
There are few to show us the relics of the past,
  But the Castle of Caerphilly calls to mind
When any foreign foe his features dare not show,
  Before Cambria felt misfortune's gales,
For Priests of that day, could fight as well as pray,
  Like Doctor Price the Grand Arch-Druid of South Wales.

The coffin was brought on a horse-drawn hearse by Edgar G. Matthews, who worked for Wilks and Powis of Pontypridd. They were also contractors for the Masters family of Lanelay Hall. The undertaker, Ebenezer Davies, was accompanied by four assistants and twelve other local men to help as bearers and they arrived at Ty'r Clettwr at 7am, where they placed the casket on a bier, borrowed from the local churchwardens.

Gwenllian and the children took one last look at the great man himself. The family and friends had remained all night to prepare for the occasion ahead. Hiarlles cut off a lock of her father's hair and kissed his face for the last time as the heavy iron casket was bolted and covered with a white pall. Gwenllian, Iesu and Penelopen left the house first. The boy was dressed in a matching foxskin hat and outfit similar to his father's costume, with breeches Vandyked at the edges, and reached to just below the knees. Hiarlles wore a traditional Welsh costume, while Penelopen wore a Welsh pais becwm and a red shawl. Gwenllian wore a long, black cloak, with tall Welsh hat. Gwenllian, affected by the sorrow of the event, was escorted by neighbour John Sparnon and Dr Anderson (the hangman's assistant) of Carmarthen.

At 8am, they reached the field at East Caerlan, close to the spot where Dr Price had cremated Iesu almost nine years earlier, and land which was owned by the doctor himself. According to the lengthy *South Wales Echo* report of the day:

"The body had been placed in a receptacle constructed of sheet iron, encircled at intervals by strong iron bands.

"This receptacle was similar in shape to any ordinary coffin.

"At the top of the lid was a square aperture disclosing the face and bust of the corpse, and those who were afforded the opportunity of gazing upon the features of the deceased declared that despite the great age, there was not a wrinkle visible in the face."

Gwenllian and the children as depicted in the South Wales Echo newspaper

111

A view of Llantrisant, with East Caerlan in the background. Notice the enormous gathering of people, there to witness Dr Price's cremation.

It seemed ironic that although the local Anglican church had condemned him for his beliefs, on the day of his funeral it was the local curate of Llantrisant Parish Church, Rev Daniel Fisher, who led the service. He was assisted by Rev J. Williams of Pontyclun, replacing the normal words of committing the body to the "earth", with that of committing it to "fire".

He read an adaptation of the service appointed for "The Burial of the Dead at Sea", saying "Yr ym ni yn rhoddi ei gorff i'r tan gan ddisgwyl am adgyfodiad y meirw ac am fywyd y byd sydd ar ddyfod". The form of the service was approved by the Bishop of the Diocese. A total of thirty-five police officers, under the eye of Supt Evan Jones, were in attendance to ensure the massed crowd remained peaceful throughout, although the service and cremation were considered "quiet".

A further fifteen constables were called to stop onlookers clambering over hedges to try to view the cremation. Chief Constable Lindsay had ordered the arrival of the police, particularly appointing Supt Jones and his assistants, Inspectors Jones of Pentre and Davies of Porth, and Sergeant Hallett.

Dr Price's cremation, showing the Price family in the centre.

The casket was placed on an iron grid above three tons of coal between two specially built walls, ten feet long, two feet thick and four feet high. More flammable material was placed on top of the grid and totally soaked in petroleum. The casket was then rested on top and lit by Dr Anderson on one end and Price's servant, Daniel Richards (Mochyn Du), with a torch on the other, at exactly 8.10am.

The site of Dr Price's cremation.

With the pyre well alight, police constables were on hand in case of any unruly crowds.

Some of the 20,000 spectators at Dr Price's cremation.

For a little time, it seemed as if the fire would not kindle, but as the mountain breezes fanned the fire and more paraffin was poured on the casket, the entire pyre was soon enveloped in flames. Thomas Forrest of the Cambrian Studio, 14 Market Street, Pontypridd, who took photographs of Price during his lifetime, was there to record the event. Journalist Morien was also present, along with historian and Town Trust Clerk Taliesin Morgan.

In fact, it was within days of Dr Price's death that Morien - no less of an eccentric himself - took hold of his pen and wrote the particularly scathing column entitled "The Late Doctor Not an Archdruid - A Protest by Morien".

It opened, "It is full time to protest against the crack-brained nonsense of attaching the title Archdruid to the name of the late Dr Price. I would refer to Dr Price with proper respect, and with the veneration demanded by his great age. But I say solemnly it is very wrong to associate his name with the venerable high priesthood of the Druidic hierarchy of this island, the great mother of all creeds.

"From time immemorial Glamorgan, the centre of the country of the bravest of the brave in ancient days - namely the Silurians - has had its Druidic sanctuary. No doubt the priests of Stonehenge retired among the Silurians during the Roman occupation and long performed their ancient religious rites at the Round Table of King Arthur and his Twelve Knights at Caerlleon-on-Usk."

THE FUNERAL PROCESSION.

The procession to the site of the cremation.

He then goes on to list the Silurian Archdruids from the year 1300 A.D. as:

Treharne Brydydd	1300	Davyd Benwyn	1560
Hywel Bach	1330	Llewelyn Shon	1580
David ap Gwilym	1360	Watcin Pywel	1620
Ieuan Hen	1370	Edward Davydd	1650
Ieuan Dew Hen	1420	Davydd o'r Nant	1680
Ieuan Gethin	1430	Samuel Jones	1700
Meredydd ap Rhosser	1470	Dafydd Hopin	1730
Ieuan Deulwyn	1480	John Bradford	1760
Iorweth Vynglwyd	1500	Iolo Morganwg	1780
Lewys Morganwg	1520	Taliesin ab Iolo	1826
Meiryg Davydd	1560	Myvyr Morganwg	1847

Morien continues to rant, "The above named carried down from age to age the marvellous lore." However, Morien was no kinder to the doctor's memory in a separate article in the same newspaper the week after his death. It read, "Wales has lost its most eccentric character, for Dr William Price is dead. He was a most peculiarly constituted man.

"That he was able as a physician is generally believed, especially by those workmen's wives who remember Dr Price in his prime. It is stated that in those days he was strikingly handsome, and as refined as a lady in all matters pertaining to his profession. Thus the women, after in their illnessess experiencing his tender and refined attentions, idolised him. Down to the time of his death his features retained striking characteristics, and old age had invested them with much dignity.

"His two eyes resembled those of a hawk; his nose was slightly aquiline in shape and his forehead was broad and lofty. He kept all his beard, and it grew in shape something similar to a goatee reaching down to his breast. It was silken and perfectly white. His hair, also white as snow, was likewise allowed to grow long, and it was plaited in long skews, the ends of which were looped up about the lower parts of his head. The shape of the head was truly magnificent, and indicated, from a phrenological point of view, great mental prowess. But his remarkable eccentricities through all periods of his long life left no doubt in the minds of those who knew him intimately that his brain was seriously affected. It seemed as if his great natural gifts were always struggling with a "mind diseased", but as far as is known, he could satisfactorily command his mind in the excercise of his profession. That he was most daring in surgery is well known, and he was more than once called to account for it: but nothing was ever proved against him."

The scene, as depicted in the South Wales Echo.

At 4pm on the cremation day, the shattered casket was found almost totally destroyed by the heat. Supt Jones and Dr Williams agreed that there was little point in placing more coal on the flames. It was placed on the bier and allowed to cool, although souvenir hunters tried to scavenge amongst the remains of the furnace. There were still 6,000 people at the site by this time, rummaging across the site and snatching pieces of cinder from the fire.

The casket was returned to Ty'r Clettwr, where the remains were placed on the couch where he had died. For years, people combed the field to find remains of him. A well-known member of Pontypridd Council related with gusto how he did a thriving trade selling the teeth of dead sheep for half-a-crown each by claiming them to be those of Dr Price.

He became a subject of poems and songs that month, with the following logged in Pontypridd library:

The Cremation of Dr Price

Doctor Price, the noted Druid,
Has now drawn his final breath,
And his voice, so clear and ringing,
Has been silenced by grim death;
Full of years he has departed;
His career was very strange.
Seldom have men's lives encompassed
Such a long and changeful range.

As he died, he called them to him,
And these words he slowly said:
"In the grave you must not lay me,
When my form is still and dead;
Let my body be consumed
By fierce flames, and let my dust
Scattered be again to Nature
All that blossoms on earth's crust."

Through the countryside this saying
Went on ever speeding wing.
Many hundreds quickly gathered
To behold this curious thing;
And on Tuesday morn at daybreak
Was his corpse with reverence borne
To Caerlan field, at Llantrissent,
Followed by sad hearts who mourn.

Thus they did as he had ordered,
And he rests in calmful peace,
As though by a grave encompassed,
Where all earthly sorrows cease;
Let us gently treat his memory -
He, a Welshman of renown -
For he loved his country dearly,
And for her sake bore many a frown.

Gwenllian Llywellyn was the executor of his Will, which was read on 20 February, 1893 and outlined the value of his personal estate at £400 5s 6d with further savings of £54 4s 5d. His Will, signed on 22 February, 1891 and countersigned by witnesses David William Davies of The Firs, Llantrisant and innkeeper Roderick Lewis of the Wheatsheaf, includes references to a series of his favourite books. They include the Cymerian Grammar, three volumes of the Archaeology of Wales, two copies of the L'Antiguite Exuliques by Bernard Montfaucen; Les Origin de Town les Cultes by Dupais, a copy of Odysseiau and Iliad by Barnes, Dr Etukely's Stonehenge and six volumes of the History of the Native Tribes of America which should not be sold after his death but given to Iesu and Penelopen and their descendants "forever, amen, amen". His breed of Glamorgan cattle, including many cows, should also be kept until his youngest child reached 21 years of age. The Will goes on to state that his estate should be left in the hands of his children and that on their death they should also be cremated within the "triangle" of Caerlan. The Will was proved at Llandaff on 20 February, 1892 by the oath of Gwenllian Llewellyn.

In 1896, just three years after Dr Price's death, an exhibition was held in his honour at Druid's Rest in the "Old Cardiff" Exhibition Building in Cathays Park as part of the Cardiff Fine Art, Industrial and Maritime Exhibition. The triumph of Empire was celebrated and inside the Indian-style exhibition pavilion, the visitors found the places of honour occupied by symbols of Britain's industrial supremacy – a model of a South African gold mine, a model coal mine, railway locomotives and coaches, hydraulic pumps, printing machine depictions of great battle victories such as Waterloo. But in an adjoining room, amidst a motley collection of minor relics, was the curiously titled exhibition, "The Late Dr Price of Llantrisant. The Famous Archdruid. Sketch of His Life and Adventures". The exhibition's contents are totally unauthentic. However, one of the most delightful aspects of the exhibits was the accompanying brochure, written by Ap Idanfryn, who wrote passionately about Price and his colourful life in quotations taken from the interviews held with the old doctor. The journalist, born Gwilym Hughes of Llanrhaiadr-yn-Mochnant (where William Morgan translated the Bible into Welsh in 1588), was the son of a schoolmaster. He went on to play an active role in the local literary circles of Cardiff, writing for *Welsh Outlook* and the *South Wales News* for more than twenty years. He died in 1933.

Ap Idanfryn's opening lines read, "There lived a man whose name is familiar to all Welshmen, and whose deeds have on more than one occasion been the theme of comment throughout the whole length and breadth of the United Kingdom. In Glamorganshire, especially, his eccentric actions and his marvellous escapades are frequently dilated upon with manifest enjoyment by some of the older inhabitants, whose memories carry them back to the troubled days of the Chartist riots. The anecdotes concerning him are innumerable and although, in their passage from mouth to mouth, some of them have been distorted out of all consistency with truth, still most of them have some foundation in fact, and it is questionable whether any one in his position in life has had a more adventurous career.

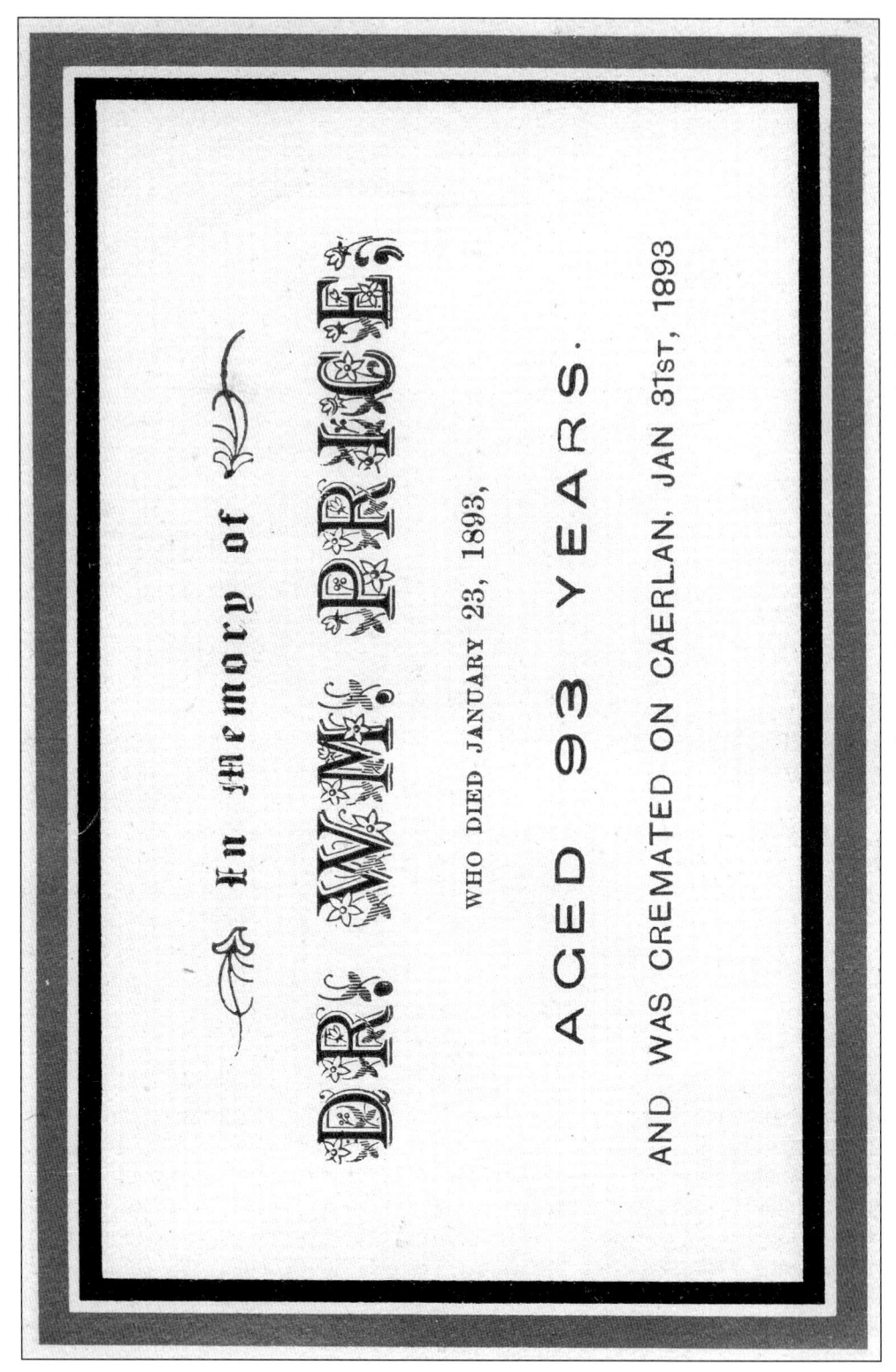

In Memory of
Dr. WM. PRICE
WHO DIED JANUARY 23, 1893,
AGED 93 YEARS.
AND WAS CREMATED ON CAERLAN, JAN 31ST, 1893

The memorial card printed by Gwenllian Llewellyn to commemorate Dr Price's death.

"In some respects he seems to have possessed attributes akin to those of Salamander, for although the mighty engines of the criminal law have several times been put in motion against him, he has never failed to elude their iron grasp. Three times has he been criminally prosecuted, but on each occasion the prosecution failed to convict him.

"It would be difficult indeed to name any subject with respect to which this extraordinary person agrees with his fellowmen. He seems to have raised his hand against the whole community and to despise all those things which mankind has learned to regard with reverence and respect. Whatever is customary is necessarily wrong; and this theory was carried out by him even in the smallest affairs of life. According to his peculiar creed, matrimony is to be mercilessly condemned as an institution which reduces the fair sex to a condition of slavery; the burial of dead bodies is a barbarous practice; and should be superseded by cremation; the eating of animal flesh has a tendency to revive in man the worst passions of a brute."

The seventeen items on show included a sketch of "The Doctor in the act of chopping off the bailiff's toes who tried to force an entrance into the house to levy a warrant for debt." This was a total fabrication and it is said that certain members of the audience shouted out in protest against the curator who attemped to courteously guide the public around the wax models and exhibits. There also were drawings of his arrest and the chest he hid in after the police came to his home in Treforest following the failed Chartist Riots – another incorrect exhibit, since he escaped from Treforest to France as a woman. He used the chest for his second escape twenty years later. According to the exhibition brochure, there were also two pistols on show which the doctor used to keep the public at bay while trying to cremate Iesu Grist, although no record is found of him ever possessing pistols on that historic day. There was also a walking stick, pictures of the cremation and the coffin, the sofa on which he died, his favourite chair, medical table and the hooked thorn which was used to pull Iesu from the flames. His costume, also shown, was later donated to the Museum of Welsh Life at St Fagans near Cardiff. Probably the most peculiar – and fake - exhibit is listed last as "The only remains of the Doctor after his cremation, viz: his right foot – it being said by scientists that the whole nature of his body must have dropped to his foot, which is on view."

During the same year, Taliesin Morgan, the Clerk of Llantrisant Town Trust, published his *History of Llantrisant*. This charming, romantic vision of the town, wholly untrustworthy as an historical document, features a small chapter on the doctor. It opens with the following amusing passage, "For many years there lived in the Town a medical gentleman of very eccentric manners known as Dr William Price. He held very peculiar views on Druidism and Cremation, and his dress had a peculiarity, in imitation of the old Welsh Druids and he posed himself as the Archdruid of Wales. In general, however, he was regarded with amused tolerance. Not of very large stature, and generally clothed in his green-cloth trousers, scalloped, his scarlet vest, green cloth jacket or shawl, with fox-skin cap, of quick movement and sharp manner was not unfamiliar in the district."

Chapter Eleven
THE LEGACY

DR WILLIAM Price's greatest legacy must surely be the passing of the Cremation Act of 1902, correctly named An Act for the Regulation of the Burning of Human Remains, and to Enable Burial Authorities to Establish Crematoria, 2nd July, 1902. His influence had a massive effect on the outcome and the reason why cremation became the alternative to burial for the dead.

Fortified by Dr Price's court hearing in 1884, the Council of the Cremation Society declared itself absolved from the promise to the Home Secretary not to use Woking Crematorium and issued a circular informing the public it was now prepared to proceed with the cremation of anyone who requested it. The Society, however, realised that it was imperative at this stage to give no cause whatever for criticism and, consequently, three conditions had to be strictly observed before a body would be accepted for cremation at Woking,

These conditions, designed to prevent the destruction of a body which might have met death illegally, continued for many years to be the only form of certification for cremation and they remain substantially the basis of the statutory forms still used at the present time.

The Council of the Cremation Society fully appreciated that some form of official regulation was needed, and on 30th April, 1884, Dr Cameron (later Sir Charles Cameron), Member of Parliament for Glasgow, introduced a Bill in the House of Commons to provide for the regulation of cremation and other means of disposal of the dead. Dr Cameron was supported by Dr Farquharson, the Member of Parliament for Aberdeen, another member of the Council, and Sir Lyon Playfair. The Bill was, nevertheless, opposed not only by the Government but also by the Leader of the Opposition. 149 voted against it, but the 79 votes in favour of it were far more than the promoters had dared hope.

On 26th March, 1885, the first official cremation at Woking took place. Mrs Pickersgill, a well known figure in literary and scientific circles, was the first of three cremations that year. Mr Charles William Carpenter was cremated on 19th October and, in December, the third cremation, even though the body of a fourteen-stone woman was again successfully performed in only $1^1/_2$ hours. In 1886, ten bodies were cremated. During 1888, in which 28 cremations took place, the Council of the Cremation Society issued a special appeal to the public for funds to carry out a plan to provide a chapel, waiting rooms and other amenities at the Woking Crematorium.

In 1891, a society had been formed in Glasgow to be known as the Scottish Burial Reform and Cremation Society. To Manchester fell the honour of providing the first crematorium in the provinces, when in 1892 a group of public-spirited citizens formed a company which built, on the south side of the city, a crematorium. Four years later, similar action was taken by a group of citizens of Liverpool, where the fourth crematorium in Great Britain was established. Back in London, the Council of the Cremation Society was seeking a site for a crematorium on the north side of London and, after many years of failure, at last succeeded in obtaining a piece of land adjacent to Hampstead Heath. In 1900, at the instigation of the Council of the Cremation Society, the London Cremation Company Limited was formed with the object of establishing a crematorium on the new-found site. The necessary funds were obtained and a distinguished architect, Sir Ernest George, R.A., was appointed to plan what was to become one of the most famous crematoria in the whole of the world, namely, Golders Green.

In the following year, the Darlington Cremation Society built a crematorium in the grounds of the public cemetery and branches of the Darlington Society were created in Sunderland and at Tyneside. It was in this year, however, that a most significant event occurred: the opening of the first municipal crematorium in Great Britain, at Hull. Until now, private individuals were, of their own accord, or acting through the medium of the Cremation Society, responsible for combating the great prejudice which cremation had encountered and also for the establishment of the four existing crematoria. Now, for the first time, a local authority had acknowledged how important it was, both socially and economically, to provide cremation services for the community.

Twenty-eight years after the abortive parliamentary efforts of Sir Charles Cameron and his friends, cremation had achieved a form of governmental regulation and it became officially recognised in the highest quarters. The new Act of Parliament gave powers to the Home Secretary to make Regulations which were published as Statutory Rules and Orders in March, 1903. It was all thanks to that one Welshman who cremated his son high on a hill.

Dr Price's family remained in Llantrisant for the remainder of their lives. In 1902, Ty'r Clettwr was demolished and Zoar Chapel was built by the members of Bethel Chapel, who departed the congregation sixty years earlier. Bethel's worshippers left their original chapel, which later became the parish church hall, for a large room at Mwyndy Farm.

Nicholas Price (1884-1963)

Caerlan House built by John Parry

Unfortunately, John Jones left the farm in 1862 and Mrs Thomas, of the Talbot Inn, offered them the long room upstairs. Eventually, they acquired, on lease, land at Cardiff Road, Penygawsi, where the first Soar was erected. In 1902, they opened the new Zoar on High Street.

Gwenllian Llewellyn accepted Christianity later in life, ensuring both of Price's children were christened, although there is no record of this taking place in Llantrisant Parish Church. She was eventually to marry John Parry of Llanharan, a Glamorgan County Council road inspector, and settled into the Butcher's Arms on Heol y Sarn, and later the White Hart on the Bull Ring. Together, they planned the house on the top of East Caerlan, in 1906. They had a daughter, called Rachel, who remained faithful to the Price children and cared for their every need. Unmarried, she stayed at East Caerlan until her death in 1985, when the house and its contents were sold at auction. In 1986, East Caerlan House sold for £57,000, with the contents selling for £12,000, and the majority of the proceeds being donated to the British Red Cross, of which both Rachel and Penelopen played a leading part, locally.

Gwenhiolen Hiarlles Morganwg Price died in 1928 at the age of eighty seven. No records remain of her and it is unlikely she had any descendants. Iesu Grist II was renamed Nicholas following Dr Price's death. A mysterious figure, Nicholas briefly married the daughter of a local farmer, Harriet Watkins, of Ty'n Llwyn Farm, but was considered a little work-shy and eventually the marriage failed. For a while, he fled the area to live in America, settling in Detroit around 1908 and therefore avoiding national service during the First World War. He was also a carpenter and builder for stonemason Will John at the RAF aerodrome in St Athan, before spending time in Newport. At one time, he was a policeman in Reading but is best remembered as a heavy drinker and bare-knuckle fighter in the streets of Llantrisant after dark.

Although immaculately dressed, he adopted some of his father's eccentricities by never wearing socks. He died in June 1963 and was cremated at Glyntaff, Pontypridd.

Nicholas Price c.1960

Penolopen Elizabeth Price (1886-1977)

Penelopen Elizabeth was a gifted musician and scholar. Brought up at the Butcher's Arms before moving to East Caerlan House, she became a qualified nurse and was recognised for her services to the Red Cross during World War I. She was best known as the local piano teacher, who would travel from home to home on horseback to give lessons. In 1909, she appeared in the National Pageant of Wales, dressed rather superbly as Britannia. On September 17, 1947, Penelopen was invited to return to the spot of her family home, now Zoar Chapel, to unveil a small bronze plaque in memory of her father, sponsored by the Royal Cremation Society. There is no mention of Nicholas or their mother Gwenllian attending the occasion. Penelopen was joined by the Lord Mayor of Cardiff, members of Llantrisant Town Trust, Councillor Ivor Jacob, Arthur Pearson MP for Pontypridd and Hugh Royle, the Chairman of the Federation of British Cremation Authorities. A crowd of more than 300 people turned out for the unveiling of Dr William Price's commemorative plaque in a town that had once persecuted him for his beliefs.

Penelopen dressed as Britannia

Present were members of the first Cremation Conference held in Wales, which took place in Cardiff over a three-day period. Children were released from the local schools to enjoy the carnival atmosphere, the centre of which was found on the stone wall near Price's old home. Coun Jacob opened the proceedings: "We are here to pay tribute to the memory of an illustrious resident of this old town," he explained, and added that the plaque was a "fitting tribute to a great man." Miss Price pulled the chord which unveiled the plaque, and said: "I am proud and happy to unveil this plaque in memory of my father and hope it will be preserved for all time"

The plaque read: "This tablet was erected by The Cremation Society and the Federation of British Cremation Authorities to commemorate the act of Dr William Price, who cremated the body of his infant son in Caerlan Fields, Llantrisant. For this act, he was indicted at the Glamorganshire Winter Assizes on the 12th February 1884, where he was acquitted by Mr Justice Stephen who adjudged that cremation was a legal act."

Penelopen and Rachel outside Caerlan House

Penelopen Price unveiling the plaque in memory of her father at Zoar Chapel, September 1947

Hugh Royle, the chairman of the Federation of British Cremation Authorities, Arthur Pearson MP and Mrs Gilbert, vice chair of the Council of Cremation Society, spoke at the event and presented Miss Price with a silver salver.

The crowd sang *Cwm Rhondda* and the Welsh national anthem *Hen Wlad Fy Nhadau*, bringing the day's events to a close. At 9.15pm that evening, a 45-minute radio play was broadcast by the BBC. Written and produced by P. H. Burton, it featured Arthur Phillips as Dr Price, Ivor Maddox as Justice Stephen and David J. Thomas as the narrator.

The cast spent 10 hours of rehearsals over three nights prior to the broadcast, which also included a speech from Lord Horder, President of the Cremation Society. It opened: "In a previous generation, Dr William Price was a figure of controversy.

" In our own day, he has become a romantic legend and around his name have been woven fantastic stories of mostly improbable deeds. Price was a courageous pioneer; one might say he was an architect of a great sanitary reform, which is today recognised by thinking people not only as desirable, but as an economic necessity."

However, probably the most important section of the broadcast was the postscript itself, written by Penelopen Price herself: "I was only five when my father died, but I have some vivid memories of him. He was such a remarkable man that anybody who met him never forgot him, and to live with him every day was a great experience for an impressionable child.

"I soon gathered that there was something different about him from other men, and I became very proud of him. When we went for a walk, men raised their hats to him, and treated him almost with reverence; I noticed that they did not raise their hats when they passed other men. Then, again, he did not dress like other men.

"He always wore green trousers, Van-dyked at the foot and edged with red silk braid; a line of red silk braid also ran down each trouser leg. His waistcoat was red, edged with green. In his younger days, he wore a green coat, but when I knew him he wore, over the waistcoat, a sort of white smock. The big brass buttons were figured with goats, and the little buttons for the waistcoat with little kids. We always kept goats, and he was very fond of them.

"On his head he wore a foxskin, and over his shoulders a big plaid shawl. Of course, he was intensely Welsh, and I did not speak a word of English until I went to school. When I was a little child, my father always insisted that I should be dressed in full Welsh costume. Naturally, I wanted to dress like other little girls, and just to please me, my mother bought me a red frock and white pinafore.

"When I wore this, I used to steal out through the cowshed and return the same way, in order to avoid meeting my father, for I would not have displeased him for the world. Not that he would have been angry. He was the most gentle of men, and did not believe in giving way to anger. Nor would he indulge in swearing. My mother never heard him use a single swear word, not even of the mildest kind.

More than 300 people turned out for the unveiling of the plaque to Dr Price.

"He was always extremely gentle with animals, and I can remember the great distress there was in the house when a favourite dog was lost; it jumped out of the window and followed my father to Cardiff. Everything possible was done to find him, but he was never found. My father was so reluctant to cause suffering to animals that he was not even willing to let my mother kill the chickens. He said they should be allowed to die naturally. He was a strict vegetarian himself and would not touch fish, flesh or fowl. He kept a herd of Glamorgan cattle to have the milk, butter and cheese for his own use. I remember once that my mother killed some young cockerels, not thinking that my father would notice, because he was 90 years old by that time, but he was still as upright as a line and his voice was not like an old man's. He noticed that the cockerels had gone and he guessed what had happened. He did not get angry, but he said with a smile to my mother, "You think I'll be dying soon, so I won't want the cockerels any longer." When my mother asked him why he wanted to keep them, he said he liked to hear them crowing in the morning. I remember that incident very well, because even though I was only a little child, I know my mother had done wrong in killing the chickens.

"I don't want to give the impression that I was afraid of my father. It would be truer to say that I almost worshipped him. Every morning, my brother and I would go in to see him and show him that our hands were clean. Then he would give a penny to each of us, but we were not allowed to spend it on sweets. I used not to jump on his lap and kiss him, as so many children do to their fathers. I used to think that he was too great to be treated with such familiarity. I remember once that a neighbour's child came in and jumped up on him and kissed him, and I felt shocked. Of course, I was wrong; children loved him and he loved them.

"My final memory of him was of his cremation. How proud I was that day! My mother, my brother and I walked behind the body between lanes of people who had come to pay their last homage. They say there were 20,000 of them. People have asked me if the sight of the fire did not frighten me. I had no such fear, because my father had said it was the right thing to do. I said I felt proud, and I still feel proud. All my life I have had to listen to fantastic stories about my father, most of them a lot of rubbish, but I suppose that such

The plaque unveiled in memory of Dr William Price

stories are the tribute that ordinary men pay to those who are greater than them. When I was a child, I thought my father was a great man. I still think so".

A year later, in December 1948, Gwenllian (Llewellyn) Parry died at the age of 89. On November 30, 1953, Penelopen opened Thornhill Crematorium and on October 8, 1966, unveiled a stained glass window in memory of her father at the North Chapel of Glyntaff. Although the cemetery at Glyntaff, close to Price's home, was opened in June 1875, the crematorium was not opened until June 1924. The new window was created by Celtic Studios in Swansea and was paid for by public subscription at a cost of £560. Miss Price never married and had no children and she died in 1977, aged 91. Her constant companion was stepsister Rachel. Most agreed that it was Penelopen who was considered the 'lady of the house', while the younger woman carried out the day-to-day running of their lives.

Almost a century after the cremation of Iesu Grist, the town of Llantrisant paid another tribute to their famous resident by unveiling a statue to him on the Bull Ring. Designed by leading sculptor Peter Nicholas of Rhoose, the statue to Dr William Price was unveiled by the Mayor of Taff-Ely Borough Council, Coun George Preston and his wife Rhoswen, in the May Day festival of 1982.

The figure shows him with arms outstretched, 'blown by the winds of adversity', wearing fox-skin hat, Druidical cloak, his left hand holding a crescent moon, the other hand holding a torch. With a sword worn around his waist, he is standing on a boulder, presumably symbolising the Rocking Stone. Peter Nicholas was invited to consider designing a commemorative sculpture for the town in the summer of 1980.

Penelope Price at the unveiling of a window at Glyntaff Crematorium

The commission came from Taff-Ely Borough, with advice from the Welsh Arts Council. The statue overlooks East Caerlan, the site of the famous cremation. Thousands of people descended on the town for the May Day Festival and Beating the Bounds ceremony, which coincided with the unveiling. Children's choirs from the three local schools combined to perform a homage to Dr Price, written by local poet Gwilym Llaeron (William Lewis) of Beddau and was sung to the tune of *God Bless the Prince of Wales*.

Homage to Dr William Price

Today we sing the praises
Of Dr William Price,
Who legalised cremation
Throughout the British Isles.
His infant he cremated
One day at East Caerlan
And thereby gained the hatred
Of almost all in Llan.

Chorus
So let us sing the praises
Of this farsighted man,
Who legalised cremation,
That day at East Caerlan.

And here on the Bull ring
In sight of East Caerlan,
Today we place a statue
In honour of this man.
He was a Welsh heretic
A queer sort of chap,
His deed that day set firmly
Llantrisant on the map.

He also was a Druid
And Chartist of renown,
This character made headlines
In cities and in town,
Dressed in quaint regalia
His cap made out of fur,
When riding through the area
He always caused a stir.

And here we are gathered
Today as you can see,
To place this fine memorial
Up to his memory.
So let us raise our voices
In song up to the skies,
And thank the Lord for sending
Us, Dr William Price.

The statue to Dr William Price, Llantrisant

The unveiling of the statue also coincided with a rather different song about Dr Price, written by members of Llantrisant Folk Club, who used his image as the symbol for their organisation.

1. There was a man called Doctor Price
   Who lived on lettuce, nuts and rice
   His idols were the moon and sun
   And walked the hills with nothing on.

2. The naughty doctor in his day
   Put lots of girls in the family way
   His little offspring could be seen
   From Pontypool to Pontyclun.

3. The Nonconformists didn't like
   The practices of Doctor Price
   They say he wasn't nice to know
   He had an enormous libido.

4. So at the age of eighty eight
   The doctor thought he'd take a mate
   He married a girl called Gwenllian
   And became the father of her son.

5. A doting dad was Doctor Price
   He called the baby 'Jesus Christ'
   He wrapped it in a flannel shawl
   The bonniest baby of them all.

6. But one year later sad to say
   The Doctor's baby passed away
   So after chapel one dark night
   He set the little corpse alight.

7. The Doctor thought it quite a joke
   To watch the kid go up in smoke
   He took the ashes with a grin
   And kept them in a biscuit tin.

8. But when the local deacons saw
   That Doctor Price had broke the law
   They shouted at him 'ach a fi'
   And put him under lock and key.

9. The Doctor told the Magistrate
   He didn't care about his fate
   'It was the most hygienic way,
   I'll be a famous man some day'.

10. The morning that the Doctor died
    His children sat at his bedside
    He drank a bottle of champagne
    And started singing once again.

11. He told his children in his will
    To burn him on Llantrisant hill
    They built a crematorium
    And the Doctor went to Kingdom Come.

12. So it's thanks to Doctor William Price
    That modern corpses have the choice
    To either linger in the mouldering clay
    Or go up the chimney straight away.

In 1994, the Dr William Price Memorial Garden, dedicated to the Welsh heretic, was unveiled by Llantrisant Community Council on the corner of High Street, directly opposite the site where Ty'r Clettwr once stood. Throughout 1996, campaigners in Caerphilly fought tirelessly to save the Green Meadow Pub, which was considered the site of the original Ty'n y Coed Cae Farm, where the doctor was born. However, this was never proved and even in interview with Penelopen Price in 1959, Dr John Cule was told the original house had been a ruin for years. Sadly, despite several attempts to save the pub, in March 1997 they lost their fight and it was demolished, to be replaced by a housing development.

Since then, industrial estates, and even buildings in the University of Glamorgan, Treforest, bear his name, as does a group of houses in Glyntaff itself. In fact, the selection of publications and articles written about him during that time is quite phenomenal, while people of Llantrisant still talk about him with a mixture of humour and an underlying sense of respect.

More than two centuries have passed since the birth of Dr William Price, but his legacy remains secured in the annals of history as one of the most extraordinary individuals ever to have lived.

Long may the memory of this man continue.

"Dr William Price was certainly a figure of high romance. It was as though a composite creature had stepped out of the pages of Old Testament history and, in his passage through the centuries, had enriched his personality from the flow of all the hidden streams of myth and legend."

Timeline

1760   Rev William Price born
1767   Mary Edmunds born in Machen
1780   Rev Price became a Scholar of Jesus College, Oxford
1781   Rev Price resigned his scholarship on January 5
1783   Rev Price received a degree of Bachelor of Arts on June 18
1785   Rev Price became a Probationary Fellow in April
1786   Rev Price received his Master of Arts degree in April. He was later elected a Full Fellow of the College
1787   Rev Price allegedly fell from his horse
1790   Rev Price married Mary Edmunds of Machen
1791   Charles Price born
1793   Elizabeth Price born
1795   William Price born, but died aged three months
1797   Mary Price born
1800   William Price born in Rudry on March 4
1804   Ann Price born
1808   Nicholas Price born, but died aged three years
1810   William sent to school in Machen
1814   William became apprentice to Dr Evan Edwards of Caerphlly
1820   William entered The London Hospital, Whitechapel
1821   William was made a Licentiate of the Society of Apothecaries. In October he was made a member of the Royal College of Surgeons
1822   Portrait of William painted by Alexander Steward

1823	William made medical adviser to the Crawshays at the Newbridge Works (Brown Lenox), setting up an early form of National Health Service
1838	William launches a campaign to protect the Rocking Stone (Y Maen Chwyf) by creating a Druidic Museum and school. He also established the first Pontypridd Co-operative Society
1839	William became a Chartist leader. He fled to France following the failed Chartist Rising in Newport
1840	William returned to Wales
1841	Rev William Price died. William became a father to Gwenhiolen Hiarlles Morganwg (Gwenllian Iarlles Morganwg or Gwenllian, Countess of Glamorgan. The mother was Ann Morgan of Pentyrch
1842	Francis Crawshay's child delivered by Caesarian section by William
1844	Mary Price died. William's plan for an eisteddfod in Pontypridd failed
1846	Burglary at William Price's home. He called four-year-old Hiarlles his "learned counsel" in the court case.
1848	William fought the Fothergill family over land at Rudry in a court case held in Bristol. His father's body was exhumed to prove insanity. At Merthyr County Court, he brought an action against his fellow practitioner, David Gwynne Owen
1850	William sued James Curtis for assaulting him
1851	William visited the International Exhibition in Cardiff in a goat-drawn carriage
1852	William tried to lay claim to the Ruperra Estate by proving Druidic inheritance rights
1853	William held a tea-party on the Rocking Stone to raise funds for the new Victoria Bridge in Pontypridd. He was later indicted for perjury at the Glamorgan Assizes
1859	William refused to surrender land to the Treforest Tramway Company. Gwenllian Llewellyn was born in Cilfynydd
1860	William built the Round Houses at Glyntaff
1861	William published a notice that Homer built Caerphilly Castle. He was later evicted from the Round Houses and fled to France
1866	William returned to Wales. Ann Morgan died
1871	William retired as surgeon to the Brown Lenox works, Pontypridd. He published his work Gwyllllis yn Nayd. Death of Charles Price. William supported the striking coalminers of Aberdare and Rhondda
1872	Death of Elizabeth Price. William moved to Ty'r Clettwr, Llantrisant.
1873	William purchased land at East Caerlan. He was acquitted of the manslaughter of Thomas Price

1874	Othello produced in Pontypridd under William's patronage
1875	William visited London and allegedly met Karl Marx
1878	Death of Ann Price
1879	William furious over re-interment of family graves at Bedwas Church
1881	William and Gwenllian "married" at the Rocking Stone
1883	Iesu Grist Price born
1884	Death and cremation of Iesu Grist at East Caerlan. Cardiff Court trial won by William, leading the way for the passing of the Cremation Act. Iesu Grist II (renamed Nicholas) was born. William later attended the Cardiff Art Exhibition and undressed down to a new Druidic outfit
1886	Penelopen Elizabeth Price born
1888	Death of Myvyr Morganwg, Archdruid of Wales. William was interviewed by journalist Ap Idanfryn.
1891	William wrote his Last Will and Testament
1892	William injured in a fall from his carriage
1893	Death of Dr William Price on January 23. His cremation attracted 20,000 people to the town
1896	William's belongings appeared in the Cardiff Exhibition
1901	Death of Dr Richard Anderson
1902	Cremation Act passed by Parliament. Ty'r Clettwr was demolished
1906	Gwenllian and her husband John Parry built a house at East Caerlan. They had a daughter, named Rachel
1921	Dead of Morien (Owen Morgan)
1928	Hiarlles Morganwg died aged 87
1947	Commemorative Plaque unveiled by Penelopen Price at Zoar Chapel
1948	Gwenllian (Llewellyn) Parry died aged 90
1953	Penelopen Price opened Thornhill Crematorium, Cardiff
1963	Death of Nicholas Price
1966	Penelopen unveiled stained glass window in Glyntaff Crematorium, Pontypridd, in memory of her father
1977	Death of Penelopen Price, aged 91
1982	Unveiling of statue to Dr William Price at Llantrisant
1985	Death of Rachel Parry
1986	East Caerlan and contents sold at auction
1994	Dr William Price Memorial Garden opened at High Street, Llantrisant
1996	Campaigners lost fight to save the Green Meadow Pub, Rudry, claiming it was the house where William was born

Bibliography

Dr William Price (1800-1893) of Llantrisant: The Study of An Eccentric, by John Cule (1960)

A Drop of Dew, by Rhys Davies, taken from Wales Vol IX No 31; (1949)

Victorian Pontypridd, by Don Powell, Merton Priory Press, (1996)

Empire and Identity: The Case of Dr William Price, by Brian Davies, from A People and Proletariat, edited by David Smith, (1980)

Pontypridd: A Town With No History But One Hell of a Past, by Prof Meic Stephens (2002)

A History of Llantrisant, by Taliesin Morgan (1896)

A History of Llantrisant, by Dilwyn Lewis (1982)

South Wales Daily Post: Interview Ap Idanfryn (1888)

The Story of Wales, by Rhys Davies (1947)

Eccentric or Visionary - Dr Price of Llantrisant, by J. P. Griffin, Journal of the Royal Society of Medicine, Volume 84 (April 1991)

A Welsh Heretic, by Islwyn Ap Nicholas (1973)

The Dictionary of Welsh Biography Down to 1940, by The Hon. Society of Cymmrodorion (1959)

The Secret of the Bards of the Isle of Britain, by Dillwyn Miles

Pioneers of Cremation - Dr William Price, by P. Herbert Jones (Cremation Society)

Gogoniant Hynafol y Cymmry, gan Myfyr Morganwg

The Doctor Who Burnt His Son, by Cyril Bracegirdle (Country Life, November 1984)

History of Pontypridd and the Rhondda Valleys, by Morien (1903)

Investiture of the Prince of Wales: Souvenir of Llantrisant Celebrations, by Dillwyn Lewis (1969)

Dr Price and Old Llantrisant, edited by Taff Ely Borough Council (1982)

Memories Recalled: The Poems of Gwilym Llaeron (1982)

The Late Dr Price of Llantrisant – The Famous ArchDruid (1896)

The Life of Dr William Price - (Lecture) by Brian Davies (2004)

Also, with gratitude to Sioned Hughes at the Museum of Welsh Life, St Fagans; Hywel Matthews at Pontypridd Library; Valerie Harris at Llantrisant Library; National Library of Wales Aberystwyth; Cardiff Central Library; Glamorgan Register. The author would like to thank John Cule for his thesis, without which this book would not have been possible. Also, to Dr Michael Jones, Gwyn & Mary Rees, Henry & Pat Alexander, Graham Mellor and Edmund Miles for allowing the author access to their private collections.

Biography

Llantrisant-born author Dean Powell is a Freeman of the town and a Trustee of Llantrisant Town Trust.

A graduate of the University of Wales College of Swansea, where he obtained a Bachelor of Arts degree in English and Welsh, Dean is the Editor of the *Pontypridd & Llantrisant Observer* and former Literary Editor of the *Western Mail*.

He has compiled five very successful photographic history books, with subjects ranging from his home town of Llantrisant to the history of music-making in the Rhondda Valleys.

A member of Treorchy Male Choir for the past sixteen years, Dean is also their publicity officer and honorary archivist and was recently the recipient of Life Membership of the Choir in recognition of his services to the organisation.

He has undertaken a series of successful tours to Australia, Canada and the USA as their tenor soloist. In 2004, he presented and performed in all 18 concerts with the Choir throughout Australia for a massed audience of more than 19,000, taking Brisbane, Perth, Melbourne and the Sydney Opera House by storm.

He also performs regularly in venues throughout the UK as a singer and guest speaker, has appeared on several commercial recordings and is frequently interviewed on radio and television, in both English and Welsh.